The Fair Trade Scandal

The Fair Trade Scandal

Marketing Poverty to Benefit the Rich

Ndongo Samba Sylla

Translated by David Clément Leye

PlutoPress
www.plutobooks.com

First published 2013 by Harmattan Sénégal as Le Scandale commerce équitable: le marketing de la pauvreté au service des riches.

First published 2014 by Pluto Press
345 Archway Road, London N6 5AA

www.plutobooks.com

British Library Cataloguing in Publication Data
A catalogue record for this book is available from the British Library

ISBN   978 0 7453 3425 7   Hardback
ISBN   978 0 7453 3424 0   Paperback
ISBN   978 1 7837 1013 3   PDF eBook
ISBN   978 1 7837 1015 7   Kindle eBook
ISBN   978 1 7837 1014 0   EPUB eBook

Library of Congress Cataloging in Publication Data applied for

This book is printed on paper suitable for recycling and made from fully managed and sustained forest sources. Logging, pulping and manufacturing processes are expected to conform to the environmental standards of the country of origin.

10   9   8   7   6   5   4   3   2   1

Typeset from disk by Stanford DTP Services, Northampton, England
Printed digitally by CPI Antony Rowe, Chippenham, UK

Dedicated to

*El Hadji Sylla, my father, who made me what I am today.
I can never thank you enough.*

Contents

List of Illustrations

Figures

Tables

Boxes

Acknowledgements

I would like to express my gratitude to three of my former professors who instilled in me the passion for research, supervised much of my work, and always encouraged me to explore unusual perspectives. These are Henri Nadel (Université Paris VII Denis Diderot), Jean-Claude Barbier (Université Paris I Panthéon Sorbonne) and Jacques Charmes (Université de Versailles Saint-Quentin en Yvelines and Institut de Recherche et de Développement). This book owes much to these encounters. Mactar Sylla helped me improve parts of this manuscript, as well as Dr Abdoulaye Diallo (Harmattan Sénégal), who edited the French version. I would like to give a special mention to my friend Moustapha Lo (Knoxville, Tennessee), for his tireless comments, for ensuring that I have the books I need, for always showing interest in the evolution of my research and for encouraging me to publish it. I benefited from the constant encouragement of Cheikh Mbacké Sokhna, Moussa Bassel and Ousmane Dieng.

This book was published thanks to the generous support of the Rosa Luxemburg Foundation (RLF) West African Office, which funded its translation. I would like to thank its Director, Dr Claus Dieter König, as well as Dr Arndt Hopfmann, Director for the Africa Department at RLF, who has taken the time to read and comment on previous drafts of this manuscript. David Clément Leye has translated the French manuscript into English, always displaying openness and professionalism. To David Castle, my editor at Pluto Press, who always had the time to give encouragement, advice and suggestions, I would like to express my gratitude.

And of course, the views expressed in this book are solely those of its author and not of the people or institutions mentioned.

Ndongo Samba Sylla

List of Acronyms and Abbreviations

FAO	Food and Agricultural Organization of the United Nations
FLO	Fairtrade Labelling Organizations International (Fairtrade International)
FOB price	free on board price (which includes all costs until the port of embarkation)
FT	abbreviation for the Fairtrade/Max Havelaar labelling organisation
GATT	General Agreement on Tariffs and Trade
GDP	gross domestic product
GFN	Global Footprint Network
HIPCs	heavily indebted poor countries
ILO	International Labour Organization
IMF	International Monetary Fund
LDCs	least developed countries
MDGs	Millennium Development Goals
MMGE	major manufactured goods exporters
MPE	major petroleum exporters
NGO	non-governmental organisation
OECD	Organisation for Economic Co-operation and Development
Oxfam	Oxford Committee for Famine Relief
PSE	producer support estimate
UN	United Nations
UN Comtrade	United Nations statistical database on international merchandise trade
UNCTAD	United Nations Conference on Trade and Development
UNDP	United Nations Development Programme
WFTO	World Fair Trade Organization
WTO	World Trade Organization

Introduction

Economic alternatives do exist. Or so we're told. 'Another' capitalism, a 'human-faced' capitalism even, is possible. Ethics can be introduced into capitalism. The market economy can be made to serve the poor. The search for profit and universal commodification of everything can be useful to humanity and the environment so long as the right steps are taken. In other words, if we believe in what some might consider as a new 'utopian socialism', capitalism can be made more accountable, and this for the greater good of the working classes of the world. Microfinance made us this promise and provided many guarantees. Most of us had taken it for granted. But we are still awaiting results, despite the democratic generosity of the idea (Bateman, 2010). Nowadays, in light of the recurring banking and financial crises that are still affecting hundreds of millions of lives, we increasingly hear about the concept of ethical financial investments. Increasingly, the goal is to make 'responsible' a global system whose peculiarity is that it does not tolerate any ethical limitation.

In its attempts to redeem the free market, rather than introduce an alternative form of globalisation, Fair Trade is perhaps the most revolutionary and hopeful initiative for workers in the poorest countries of the planet. Its supporters want to put an end to unequal exchange between North and South. They argue that poor workers of the South should enjoy decent prices for what they sell to rich countries. To achieve this, they promote militant activism, namely awareness-raising campaigns, as well as solidarity from consumers in the North. In theory, agreeing to pay a slightly higher price for some goods made from raw materials produced in the South could contribute to improving the living conditions of workers of the South through the Fair Trade networks.

The fact that Fair Trade has achieved a significant impact in some regions of the world is undeniable. But isolated and limited successful experiences are insufficient to argue that this tool has been effective in reforming capitalism. As we will demonstrate in this book, Fair Trade is a new iteration of the free market rationale, rather than an alternative to the market economy. Contrary to what some of its neoliberal critics argue, Fair Trade is a logical continuation of free trade and not a remedy to its weaknesses. The reason for this is quite simple. Can the excesses of the market economy be overcome using the same principles and methods? Can the grip of the free market on human lives actually be loosened while still promoting further trade, albeit in innovative ways? The answer is most certainly no.

Fair Trade nevertheless seeks to change the world by extending the empire of commodities further. How can it do so? Poverty itself has become a commodity. Poverty is being labelled. Through this label, it is the idea and the approach that are being sold. The label gives poverty a visibility it did not have before. It gives it an identity. A seal is applied on commodities produced by the poor – in fact by a minority among the poor – so that consumers of the North can distinguish between the 'Fair' approach and others. In theory, this label guarantees that the higher price paid will be put to good use and benefit impoverished workers. But Fair Trade needs advertising in order to attract clients, as all sellers do. Marketing and awareness campaigns are necessary to promote its cause.

Putting poverty and the truth about unequal exchange at the forefront of the global public scene is quite a commendable approach. This is not what is at issue. I do not challenge the sincerity and ambition of this approach, nor the purity of its motives. The fundamental question is the following: has Fair Trade kept its promise? Is it a tool that can really help the poor of the world? Indeed, if placing a label on global poverty was enough to eliminate it, there would hardly be any reasons to disapprove of Fair Trade. The problem is that things are not quite what they seem. Between intentions and outcomes, there is a gap, often filled only with rhetoric.

As I shall demonstrate, Fair Trade is but the most recent example of another sophisticated 'scam' by the 'invisible hand' of the free market. This noble endeavour for the salvation of the free market was tamed and domesticated by the very forces it wanted to fight. With its usual efficiency, the free market triggered the implosion of the Fair Trade universe and hijacked its mission, without Fair Trade supporters and stakeholders even realising it. The free market was especially cunning in letting these celebrate their perceived victories with glee and carelessness, while it secretly and relentlessly pushed on with its dark designs.

Only a few years ago, I knew little about Fair Trade, despite some measure of interest in issues related to international trade. Until then, I was mostly concerned with other aspects of development. In 2010, I was fortunate to work as a consultant for Fairtrade Labelling Organizations International (FLO, which later became Fairtrade International), a result of chance as well as individual choices. To start with, I felt enthusiastic, partly because of a bias in favour of the original ideas. In the West African context where

I worked, Fair Trade was barely keeping its promises. For older producer organisations, there were initially significant benefits; then, hardly anything followed. Newcomers to the system were still waiting for promises to come true. For those who wanted to join the movement, it was sometimes an obstacle course.

It was difficult to make definitive statements about Fair Trade, however, because what little information existed was insufficient, context-specific and therefore impossible to draw any general lessons from. Besides, being reluctant to give way to praxis and empiricist judgement, I could not be satisfied with such contextual conjectures, nor with arguments heard here and there. So I immediately decided to do some research on the issue in order to reach a personal understanding and assess the theoretical potential of this solidarity approach. I naturally turned to the economic literature and to some sociological works. My research did not overlook the broad range of writings by Fair Trade actors. I also collected views from my colleagues about some aspects on which my thirst for knowledge was still unquenched. Based on this research, and on my own direct experience, I came to better understand the structure of Fair Trade and the difficulties faced by producer organisations involved in this movement. However, while I was bemused by the large number of cookbooks and promotional materials on Fair Trade, I was disappointed by what I read overall.

Let us start with the books written by the two 'founding fathers', Frans van der Hoff, a Dutch priest and economist living in Mexico, and his fellow countryman Nico Roozen, Director of the *Solidaridad* non-governmental organisation (NGO). They present a wealth of information on the genesis of the movement, the difficulties encountered and a *pro domo* advocacy. Compared with other works listed below, the founders' texts have the merit of providing, with much sincerity and honesty, theoretical arguments as well as some attempts at justification and an ideological stance. However, the most demanding readers are left disappointed by the fact that the litany of good intentions and ambitions is given more consideration than scientific discussion.

Then we have summary works that present the state of the art on Fair Trade. Their authors review the history of the movement, its mission, actors and *modus operandi*, while also expressing light criticism of the inequalities of international trade. These works implicitly argue that Fair Trade promotes something radically different against the neoliberal system. At times, the existence of divergences is alluded to with delicate caution. But the tone remains careful and any asperities are ironed out. As a result, readers seeking a contradictory perspective on Fair Trade will remain dissatisfied.

The next category is that of monographs, either in book or article form. This category contains anything and everything. For some, Fair Trade is successful and must be encouraged. For others, it is but a chimera that we should not waste time on. Others are more nuanced and argue that Fair Trade has an undeniable potential, but needs to make adjustments in order to fully become the alternative paradigm it seeks to be. Let us also mention authors whose sole intention is to demonstrate that Fair Trade can be 'modelled' and understood using the axioms and tools of the dominant economic theory. Despite this variety, these monographs have a major weakness: they tend to generalise results and make recommendations on the basis of information whose validity is *a priori* local. Besides, they eschew the global functions of Fair Trade.

Then we have critical writings and other pamphlets. In this category, one set of arguments of principle is opposed to another set of arguments of principle. On either side, a given ideological stance is backed by carefully selected empirical data. Neither side is particularly wrong or entirely right. Readers are therefore likely to make up their minds based on their own personal standpoint. This often derives from lack of a clear analytical framework.

Finally, there are speeches, writings and publications by Fair Trade actors, those who run the movement, including labelling initiatives. This gives a completely different picture, where every detail is painted in pink or in black, depending on whether it serves the objectives of the movement or not. This kind of material includes extremely sophisticated rhetoric. Statements regarding the ambitions, scope and results of this model are as pompous as they are devoid of evidence. On the inequities kindled by neoliberal globalisation, the arguments are virulent and keep up with the times. When addressing the problems faced by the world's poor, the tone is at once dark and optimistic, hence reaching out to various audiences (consumers, solidarity movements, alterglobalists, politicians, etc.). In other words, when neoliberals talk about rights, choice and freedoms, Fair Trade actors use words such as 'consum'actors', 'ethical consumption', 'responsible consumption', 'corporate social responsibility', 'sustainable development', 'a cart, a vote', 'buycott', etc.

While these materials are rich, it is difficult to extract any substance from them, or any arguments that are free from partisan ornaments. This type of literature is filled with confusing information, contradictory statements and academic laziness: philosophers arguing that consumers have a moral imperative to buy Fair Trade products, while governments are morally bound to back the movement; social scientists not paying due attention to the specificities of the contexts under study; confused economists relying on the authority of simplistic theoretical arguments provided by economic textbooks; priests being seduced by marketing; marketing gurus being satisfied with statistics they do not understand; supporters of free trade ignoring the fact that free trade has more similarities to than differences from Fair Trade; the alterglobalist movement attempting to redeem the free market ... But the greater irony is that the new advocates of the poor unknowingly work for the rich, being themselves part of this category. They proudly boast growth rates that are supposed to put to shame any previous attempts at trade solidarity while overlooking the more meaningful figures.

It is not my intention to explain this current state of the literature on Fair Trade. I can only point out that the weight of ideology, the power of marketing and the lack of evaluation data must have played an important part. Each contributed a personal perspective. All participants in this debate – including the founding fathers, researchers, pamphleteers, marketing organisations and political actors – have found or defended arguments they considered true about Fair Trade. This is the reason why some efforts at analytical clarification are required. It is also worth pointing out that Fair Trade actors have begun producing some materials which, although incomplete and diverse, help in making a thorough and honest assessment of the model they promote.

The need to study Fair Trade also arises from current affairs. As part of the ongoing multilateral negotiations – the Doha development round – the issue of trade preferences being given to the poorest countries is regularly debated, as are the effects of the obvious protectionism of rich countries on the main commodities exported by developing countries. From my point of view, Fair Trade is a low-level experiment whose study can provide precious teachings on the potential distributive effects within developing countries of the liberalisation of commodities, especially agricultural products.

This book aims to provide a critical study of Fair Trade with a dual perspective. It first provides a more analytical approach by identifying the key aspects involved and attempting to clarify the main arguments and concepts. Then it gives more weight to the not necessarily homogeneous viewpoint of the countries of the South. The focus is put especially on the least developed countries (LDCs). Indeed, one of the limits of existing literature is that it addresses the issue of Fair Trade mainly from the perspective of countries of the North (perception of the movement by consumers, tensions and controversies linked to the ideological evolution of Fair Trade, competition between labels, etc.). This bias is understandable, as Fair Trade is in a way a Western 'invention' whose survival depends on its uptake by consumers and political actors of the North. However, Fair Trade is too important an issue to be confined within the borders of developed countries. Other voices need to be heard. The bias in this debate has resulted in the heterogeneous nature of developing countries being downplayed, and a lack of attention to the progressive and distributive nature of this new development tool.

Is Fair Trade a model that can be applied to all developing countries? Is it a long-term strategy that can be recommended for these countries? Does it not hide new forms of exploitation of the South by the North? Who is benefiting from it in the South? Finally, is it a credible alternative to neoliberal globalisation?

These are the questions on which I intend to provide an empirical and analytical contribution. This book in no way seeks to answer all the questions raised by Fair Trade. It rather seeks to focus on few aspects I consider crucial, while allowing readers to gain a broader perspective. There is no doubt that a great deal can still be learnt from social scientists and legal experts on this subject.

Let us clarify the terminology. As we shall see, there are several trends in Fair Trade. Generally speaking, we have historic/alternative Fair Trade on the one hand and labelled Fair Trade on the other. This research focuses mainly on the latter approach. Indeed, when speaking about Fair Trade in general, everyday consumers think of the supermarket model. In actual fact, 'labelled Fair Trade' does embody the sociological and economic dimensions of the global Fair Trade movement. Thus, in order to avoid any confusion, every time historic/alternative Fair Trade is referred to this will be made clear. In other cases, I shall use indifferently the term 'Fair Trade' to refer to the Max Havelaar or Fairtrade approach (this latter specific approach being abbreviated as FT). It is worth pointing out that, in spite of the more widespread use of the phrase 'labelled Fair Trade', it would not be inaccurate, and may even be thought-provoking, to speak about 'Trade Labelled Fair', in order to introduce a sense of tension and to reverse the burden of proof. Why should we accept outright that the Fair Trade approach – labelled or not – is fair?

In the same way, I shall speak of 'protagonists' of Fair Trade to refer to the people and institutions that organise the movement (including the founding fathers, labelling initiatives and influential organisations). These are different from 'supporters', who back the movement worldwide. In another register, we would have spoken of party 'officials' as opposed to 'activists' or sympathisers. But the literature on the new social movements shows us that these hierarchical relations no longer adequately describe the structure of contemporary social movements. This work will consider this a theoretical assumption that requires proof whenever possible. In this respect, further research would be useful. At any rate, our basic assumption is that protagonists and supporters of Fair Trade do not all have the same motivations and agenda.

The following approach will be implemented. Chapter 1 describes the background of the problem that Fair Trade seeks to resolve: how and to what extent can the international trade system be considered unfair vis-à-vis the poor of this world?

Chapter 2 describes the inner workings of Fair Trade as well as the divergences existing within the movement.

Chapter 3 covers the main arguments of the ideological debate around Fair Trade.

The last two chapters address the question of whether Fair Trade is a solution to poverty in the South and if it really is an alternative to neoliberalism.

Chapter 4 describes and discusses the economic model on which Fair Trade is based, focusing on its limitations when it comes to reducing poverty in the South, as well as on the issue of its local impact.

Chapter 5 addresses the global impact of this movement. Indeed, there is often a major confusion between the local impact and the global impact of Fair Trade. This is unfortunate. It is by examining the functions of the movement on a global level that the main argument of this book is made, namely that Fair Trade is based on a plutocratic logic: speaking on behalf of the poor, but really being at the service of the less poor and the richer. In some way, Fair Trade needs the poor more than the poor need Fair Trade.

1

On the Inequalities of the International Trade System

It is a very common clever device that when anyone has attained the summit of greatness, he kicks away the ladder by which he has climbed up, in order to deprive others of the means of climbing up after him. In this lies the secret of the cosmopolitical doctrine of Adam Smith, and of the cosmopolitical tendencies of his great contemporary William Pitt, and of all his successors in the British Government administrations.

Any nation which by means of protective duties and restrictions on navigation has raised her manufacturing power and her navigation to such a degree of development that no other nation can sustain free competition with her, can do nothing wiser than to throw away these ladders of her greatness, to preach to other nations the benefits of free trade, and to declare in penitent tones that she has hitherto wandered in the paths of error, and has now for the first time succeeded in discovering the truth. (Friedrich List, 1885 [1841]: Fourth Book, ch. 33)

For alterglobalist movements, including Fair Trade actors, the low level of economic development noted in many regions of the world derives to a large extent from the asymmetric rules of globalisation in its current form (on this concept, see Michalet, 2004). Hence this chapter addresses the following issue: to what extent can we argue that the international trade system is unfair and biased against developing countries? We shall see that the notion of 'fairness', as generally used by alterglobalist movements, can be tackled from two perspectives. Looked at from the point of view of its consequences, namely its distributive impact, international trade did not prove to be the expected tool for redistribution and catch-up. From the perspective of processes, the rules and practices that structure them have not been fair towards the poorest countries.

The concept of 'developing country' encompasses the poor countries of the world, poverty being measured by indicators such as gross domestic product (GDP) per capita or other composite indices. Although they share many similarities, developing countries also constitute a very heterogeneous universe. Many criteria, such as geographical location, the level of economic development, trade structure, geographical specificities or the degree of economic vulnerability are features that distinguish between them (see Box 1.1). This book focuses to a large extent on the least developed countries (LDCs). In light of the specificities and problems they face in the current globalisation, they represent a group whose situation is a major source of concern. According to the United Nations Conference on Trade and Development (UNCTAD, 2010a), the LDC category is defined on the basis of three criteria: (1) low income; (2) weakness of human resources (in the areas of nutrition, health and education) and (3) economic vulnerability (vis-à-vis natural shocks, trade shocks, and also exposure to shocks, the small size of the economy and economic isolation).

Table 1.1 Developing countries

	Africa	Latin America and Caribbean	Asia	Oceania	Total
Developing countries*	53	30	27	12	122
Upper middle income*	9	20	3	3	35
Lower middle income	15	9	17	8	49
Low income	29	1	7	1	38
Major petroleum exporters	8	3	11	0	22
Major manufactured goods exporters	0	2	10	0	12
Emerging economies	0	5	5	0	10
Newly industrialised economies	0	0	8	0	8
LDCs	33	1	10	5	49
HIPCs	33	5	2	0	40
Landlocked countries	15	2	5	0	22
Small island states	5	10	2	12	29
GDP per capita (current 2008 $)	1,593	7,189	2,894	2,540	3,107
% world GDP (nominal)	2.5	6.7	18.4	0.04	27.6
% world population	14.6	8.5	57.2	0.14	80.5
% world labour force	12.1	8.5	58.6	0.12	79.4
Urbanisation rate (%)	39.6	78.7	40.3	22.6	44.2

Note: * As defined by the World Bank.
Source: UNCTAD (2010b).

Box 1.1   Developing countries

The term 'underdeveloped' was previously used to refer to countries that had not yet reached the development level of wealthy Organisation for Economic Co-operation and Development (OECD) countries, and which are also different from Eastern and Central European countries or the former Soviet bloc states (known as 'economies in transition'). Nowadays, we use the concept of 'developing countries'. In spite of the structural specificities they have in common, developing countries make up a very heterogeneous universe. In order to accommodate this heterogeneity, several classifications are available. Here I refer only to those that are the most widely used (see Table 1.1).

The first approach, at once the most basic and most widespread, consists in classifying countries on the basis of geographical location.

The second approach, as used by the World Bank, differentiates developing countries based on the gross national income per capita: upper middle-income countries (between $3,946 and $12,195 per capita), lower middle-income countries (between $996 and $3,945 per capita) and low-income countries ($995 per capita or less).

The third approach, developed by UNCTAD, identifies groups of developing countries that are defined through their foreign trade structure or their economic dynamism: major petroleum exporters (those for which oil exports account for at least 50 per cent of export revenue); major manufactured goods exporters (those for which manufactured products account for at least 50 per cent of export revenue); emerging countries; newly industrialised countries (a group which includes first-generation and second-generation countries).

The last approach, especially used by the United Nations, distinguishes between four categories of developing countries that deserve particular attention on account of their geographical location (landlocked countries and small islands) or their great vulnerability (LDCs and heavily indebted poor countries [HIPCs]).

The notion of 'development' has often been criticised, namely on account of its ethnocentric biases. This work refers to it on a regular basis, not because I find it especially heuristic, but because it still has no substitute with the same cognitive resonance.

Source: OECD (2008).

According to World Bank development indicators, the 49 LDCs account for 12 per cent of the world population and less than 1 per cent of the world's GDP. They are mostly found in sub-Saharan Africa and, to a lesser extent, in South Asia. These are essentially rural countries – with 71 per cent of the population still living in the countryside – and heavily dependent on agriculture, which accounts for close to a quarter of their GDP. In spite of the efforts that were made to achieve Millennium Development Goals (MDGs), poverty remains chronic in these countries and is especially widespread in rural areas. Fifty per cent of the sub-Saharan population lives below the international poverty threshold of $1.25 per day. For South Asia, the corresponding figure is 40 per cent (World Bank, 2010a). Unlike in developed countries, poverty in LDCs results more from underemployment and the prevalence of unproductive jobs, rather than from unemployment. Indeed, men and women from poor countries who live and work in rural areas typically have the highest levels of activity in the world. According to estimates by the International Labour Organization (ILO), there were respectively 275 million and 168 million workers in 2007 living with less than $1.25 per day in South Asia and sub-Saharan Africa. Thus, just over two-thirds of the poor workers in the world are concentrated in these two regions (ILO, 2010).

International Trade: A Lever for a Minority, a Handicap for the Majority

Due to obstacles to the international movement of labour and to imperfections linked with the free flow of capital, international trade remains practically the sole instrument for economic catch-up available to developing countries in this current globalisation. According to the traditional theory of international trade (the Heckscher–Ohlin–Samuelson model in particular), the international trade of goods is a substitute for the movement of labour. With international openness and given the differences in factor endowment (land, labour, capital, etc.), countries will tend to specialise in the production and export of goods for which they have a *comparative advantage*. Thus, in countries where labour is the abundant factor, which is the case for developing countries, exports will include a strong labour component, especially unskilled. In contrast, in countries where capital is the abundant factor, as is the case for developed countries, exports will contain a strong capital component. Trade openness therefore enables developing countries to export unskilled labour in the form of goods. This tends to increase the level of income for their unskilled labour via an increased global demand for the goods they produce. Under specific assumptions, this model even predicts an equalisation of factor prices for nations that engage in international trading, following the principle of specialisation based on comparative advantage. Another advantage of trade openness, highlighted this time by the new theory of international trade, is that it helps make substantial economies of scale and scope. This being said, did international trade actually play the role of economic lever, as predicted?

Thanks in part to the gradual lowering of tariff barriers and to enhanced commercial integration of countries in the framework of free trade zones or customs unions, international trade (total of exports and imports of goods and services measured in constant prices) increased by a factor of 18 between 1960 and 2007 (see Figure 1.1).

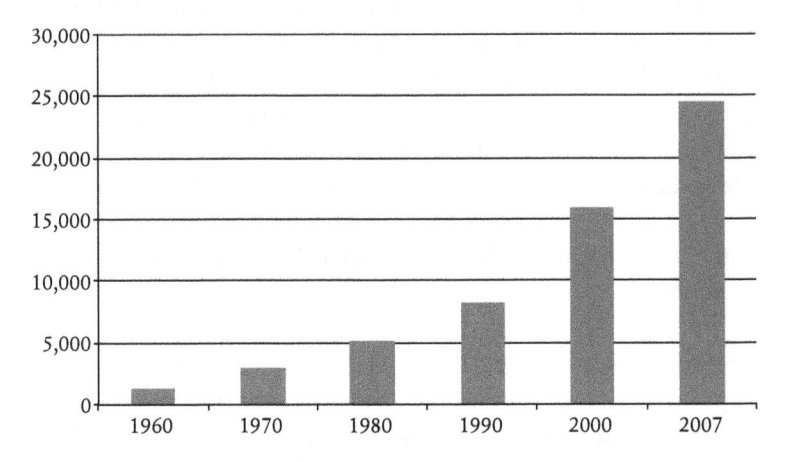

Figure 1.1   Evolution of world merchandise trade (in billions, constant 2000 $)

Source: World Bank (2010a).

On a global scale, the trade/GDP ratio rose from 24 to 58 per cent. This colossal growth of international trade represented a tremendous opportunity for developing countries to begin to catch up with rich countries. On average, their share of world merchandise exports grew from 24.5 to 38.7 per cent between 1960 and 2008, while their share of the world's GDP doubled, going from 13.5 to 26.6 per cent between 1970 and 2008. Seen from this angle, international trade has had a positive impact on developing countries (see Figures 1.2 and 1.5). However, such statistics hide significant disparities between developing countries and between geographic areas. In actual fact, only a minority managed to make it thanks to the leverage power of international trade. They are for the most part the main exporters of manufactured goods.[1] These twelve countries account for a quarter of world merchandise exports and for two-thirds of merchandise exports from developing countries. For the rest, international trade has no doubt increased in volume and value, but at a lesser rate than average. Hence, the poorest countries have become increasingly marginalised from world trade since the 1960s. Africa's share of world merchandise exports, for instance, decreased from 6 to 3.4 per cent. This trend can generally be observed in LDCs (see Figures 1.3 and 1.4). Seen from this new angle, international trade has rather heightened the development gaps. As we can note from Figure 1.5, the contribution of LDCs to world GDP remained almost unchanged over these last four decades. Among developing countries therefore, only the main exporting countries of manufactured goods have managed to close the economic gap.

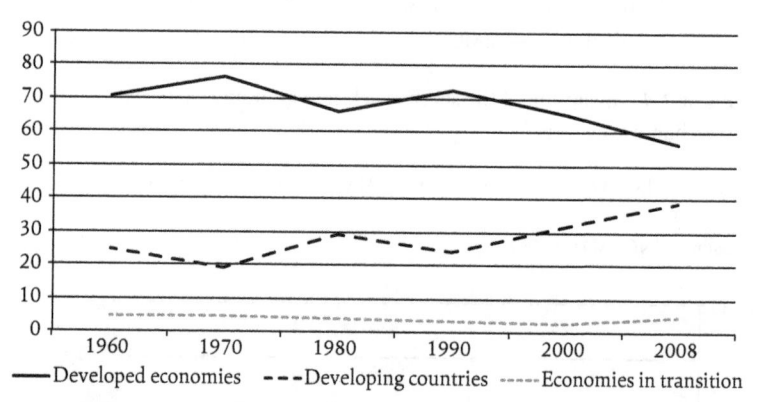

Figure 1.2 Evolution of world merchandise exports according to development status (%)

Source: UNCTAD (2010b).

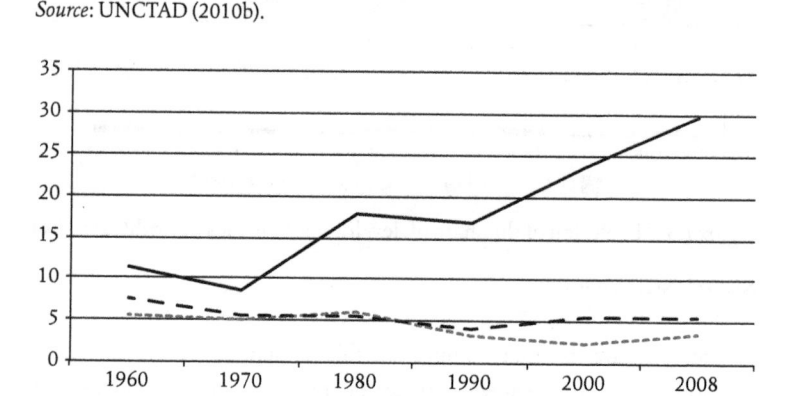

Figure 1.3 Evolution of the share of developing regions in world merchandise exports (%)

Source: UNCTAD (2010b).

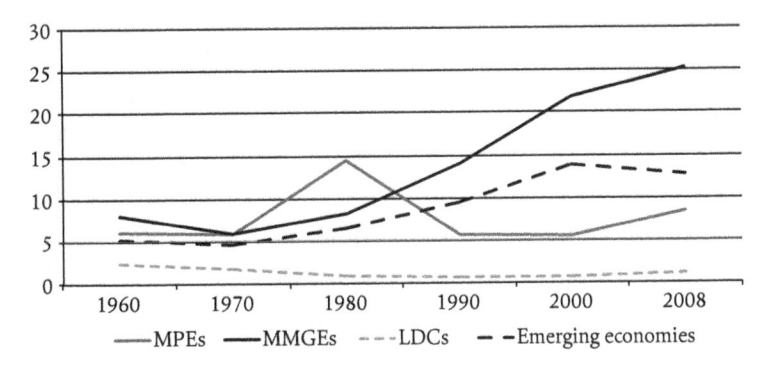

Figure 1.4   Evolution of the share of selected groupings in world merchandise exports (%)

Note: MPEs – major petroleum exporters; MMGEs – major manufactured goods exporters

Source: UNCTAD (2010b).

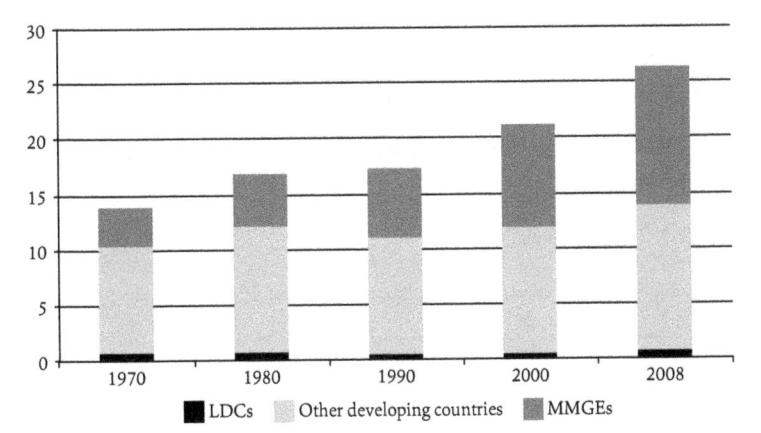

Figure 1.5   Evolution of the share of developing countries in world GDP (%)

Source: UNCTAD (2010b).

The paradox is that, alongside this economic marginalisation, developing countries showed greater openness to and dependency on international trade. Historically, most of the countries that are poor today have always been commercially open and dependent, due to their status as former colonies. In the 1970s, when these had for the most part achieved political independence, Africa was the most open/dependent region in the world. Forty years later, these trends have been heightened

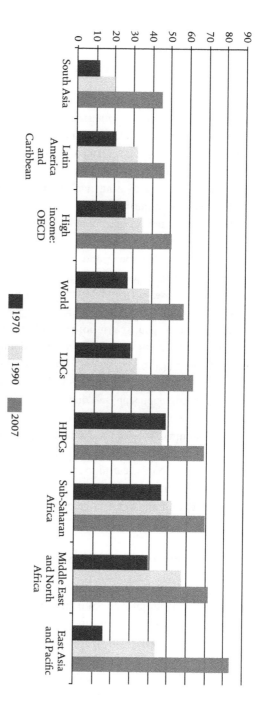

Figure 1.6   Evolution of the trade/GDP ratio (%)

Source: World Bank (2010a).

in all developing regions. LDCs – symbols of this growing openness/ dependency vis-à-vis international trade – recorded an increase in the trade/GDP ratio, moving from 30 to 62 per cent between 1960 and 2007 (see Figure 1.6). The question we can therefore ask is: why did international trade prove a handicap rather than a lever for the majority of developing countries? Why did the growing integration of the poorest countries into global trade result in their economic marginalisation?

The Problem with Primary Specialisation: A Look Back on Unequal Exchange

This economic marginalisation of LDCs is due in a large part to their low level of economic diversification, which results in a concentration of exports around a limited number of primary products and a dependency of export revenue (and often fiscal revenue) on these primary products. Such products include three categories: basic agricultural products, fuels and mining products (minerals, metals, precious stones).

The UNCTAD defines a country as 'dependent' on primary products when the export of primary products amounts to at least 50 per cent of the total export revenue. Between 2003 and 2006, 103 developing countries matched this definition. Within this group, 46 countries were dependent upon a single primary product for at least half of their export revenue (UNCTAD, 2008a: ch. 2). Even if it is true that this dependency relates mostly to mining and oil products, it is still the case that many developing countries are dependent on the export of agricultural products. The flagship products are generally coffee, cocoa, sugar, bananas and cotton (FAO, 2004).

A symptom of underdevelopment, this primary specialisation is not a fatal outcome that would relentlessly undermine the chances of economic progress. History has shown that most of the rich countries today – the United States being the most obvious example – were exporting primary products just before the First World War (Bairoch, 1995 [1993]). However, such specialisation proved harmful to the long-term interests of developing countries, as the international trade system has never before penalised the export of primary products to this extent.

Slow growth of primary product markets

For many decades, the trends have been that the trade of manufactured products developed while the trade of primary products decreased.

Indeed, between 1980 and 2009, the share of manufactured products in international commodity trade grew from 54 to 67 per cent. In the meantime, the share of agricultural products dropped from 15 to 9 per cent (WTO, 2010). As for mining and oil products, their share has also tended to drop over the long term, even though they have undergone a boost in the last few years, namely with the upsurge in the price of oil in 2008. In fact, most countries that have managed to take advantage of the development of international trade to boost their economy are those that succeeded in specialising in the export of manufactured products.

Low returns and high volatility

The decline in market shares for primary products in favour of manufactured products is revealing of a wider long-standing trend: the decline in the relative price of basic products, namely agricultural products. The assumption of a long-standing decline in the price of agricultural products compared with the price of manufactured products was put forward in the 1950s by the economists Raúl Prebisch and Hans Singer. It is in fact one of the main arguments of the theory on unequal exchange, a concept which in turn was made popular by Arghiri Emmanuel (1972 [1969]). According to the Food and Agricultural Organization (FAO, 2004), the real prices of basic agricultural products dropped by an average of 2 per cent per year between 1961 and 2001. In relative terms, the prices of agricultural products exported by LDCs dropped by 70 per cent compared with manufactured products imported from developed countries in the same period. For non-oil-producing African countries, the cumulative effect of this deterioration in the terms of trade was estimated at 119 per cent of GDP in the period 1970–97 (World Bank, 2000). The irony is that these countries, whose export revenue declined, are the very same ones that became heavily indebted, experienced problems with their trade balance and eventually bore the brunt of structural adjustment policies under the auspices of the International Monetary Fund (IMF) and the World Bank.

In addition to their low return, primary products have another main specificity: they are the products with the most volatile price in international trade. This price instability is especially pronounced for basic agricultural products. This is increasingly heightened by the 'financialisation' of the market for primary products. In other words, price evolution is less and less dictated by changes in the relation between supply and demand. Investors/speculators increasingly consider primary products as alternative financial 'assets', as they are not interested in the physical volumes traded but motivated rather by a desire to diversify their portfolio (UNCTAD, 2009: ch. 2).

It is worth pointing out that price fluctuations can sometimes have a devastating effect on production and income. For example, between 1997 and 2001, coffee prices dropped by nearly 70 per cent, stabilising below the production cost in many countries. In real terms, the 2001 price was lower than that recorded in the 1970s (FAO, 2004: 10). It is also interesting to point out that the cycles of basic product prices tend to be asymmetrical. First of all, the cycles where prices are in decline generally last longer than those where prices increase. Also, during downward cycles, price drops are more significant than the following price increases that occur when the cycle reverses. Besides, basic agricultural products are more volatile in terms of price when they are exported by developing countries than by developed countries (FAO, 2004).

Weak transmission of international prices to producers

Another specificity of the international trade of primary products is that the prices determined on the global market are imperfectly transmitted to producers in the South, who generally only receive a small percentage of it. The example of coffee is quite telling in this respect. Over the last few decades, coffee consumption has soared in developed countries. This translated into an increase in the value added of this sector. In the meantime, the prices received by producers in the South have experienced a decline. How can one make sense of this 'Coffee Paradox' – to use the expression referring to the disconnect between prices received by producers in the South and those paid by consumers in the North?

Some time ago, this situation could partly be explained by the export taxes as well as the price stabilisation mechanisms introduced by the governments of developing countries. This is less and less the case, following agricultural liberalisation policies implemented widely following structural adjustment programmes. Since then, developing countries significantly reduced the restrictions they impose on agricultural and manufactured products (World Bank and IMF, 2009).

This is one of the merits of the global value chain analysis[2] – to highlight recent developments on the commodity markets (agricultural and non-agricultural). The concept of the 'value chain' refers to all the steps that make up the cycle of products, from production to consumption. In fact, the global value chain (GVC) approach is especially opposed to the traditional orthodox vision, whereby product markets are considered a typical example of competitive market, with homogeneous products, a large number of small buyers and sellers, the absence of entry barriers, and relations between sellers and buyers that are supposed to be limited to on-the-spot financial transactions. Besides the fact that this perfect competition model ignores the existence of large actors in the developing countries (state marketing boards for instance), it does not adequately describe the current evolution of the relations between producers, intermediaries and consumers.

According to the GVC approach, commodity exports from developing countries increasingly occur within value chains where intermediaries seek to increase their share of the pie in order to achieve greater profit. Intermediaries wield strong market power which they exercise by controlling the market and defining steps in the value chain that are likely to be the most profitable. Their market power has been enhanced by two major trends. First, at each step, the number of actors tends to drop considerably, due to competition. This is what is called 'horizontal concentration'.

Second, actors that have specialised in specific steps of the chain tend to broaden their activities in other steps of the chain. Firms, for instance, tend to work more and more with producers in the framework of long-term relationships. This is what is called 'vertical integration'. With the help of trade liberalisation, oligopolies and oligopsonies therefore tend to become standard elements in value chains (see Box 1.2).

For these intermediaries, more particularly distribution channels and large agrifood multinationals, the strategy is twofold: on the one hand reducing costs upstream as much as possible and on the other creating value added downstream. The pressure to reduce costs is conveyed all along the value chain. It is often passed on to producers/wage workers. This then often leads to a violation of their rights and a repression of trade unions that can sometimes lead to murder (see, for example, the report by the NGO Actionaid, 2007). The pressure to reduce costs can also translate into savings at other steps upstream (transport costs for instance). A method for creating value added consists in differentiating products destined to consumers by adding 'symbolic' and 'customised' attributes to basic products purchased from producers in the South. 'Symbolic' attributes are based on reputation and marketing labels. In contrast, 'customised' attributes refer to the interpersonal component (consumption in a café, in a restaurant, etc.) which occurs during the sale of the product (Daviron and Ponte, 2005). This strategy thus makes it possible for a price decline in the South to occur simultaneously with a boost in sales in the North.

Box 1.2 Vertical integration and horizontal concentration
in the cocoa value chain

In 2008, world cocoa imports were estimated at $13 billion against $15 billion for exports (according to UN Comtrade). Côte d'Ivoire (20.3 per cent), the Netherlands (18.5 per cent) and Indonesia (9.6 per cent) are the world's three largest exporters. The world's three main importers are: the Netherlands (12.9 per cent), the United States (12.8 per cent) and Germany (10.7 per cent). Cocoa is the main source of income for 14 million producers, three-quarters of whom live in Africa. This is a perfect example of the trends in terms of vertical integration and horizontal concentration in the agricultural value chains.

At the local level: the example of Cameroon

Cameroon is the 10th largest exporter of cocoa in the world, with 2.4 per cent of market share. Regarding shipments, 60 per cent of exported volume is conveyed by four traders. Regarding purchases, ADM, Cargill and Barry-Callebaut purchase 95 per cent of the cocoa exported by this country. Local processing companies and exporting companies are increasingly integrated into the multinationals of the sector. For example, the local processing company, the Société Industrielle Camerounaise des Cacaos, is owned by Barry-Callebaut. Increased concentration and integration at the level of exports result in two factors: limited access of local exporters to capital; economies of scale associated to the 'bulk loading' of large quantities of cocoa.

At the international level

Intermediaries operate at five main points: (1) international trade – sales and purchases of cocoa beans and semi-processed goods; (2) processing of cocoa (into butter, powder or liquor); (3) the manufacturing and supply of industrial chocolate (which is the base product used to manufacture refined chocolate products); (4) the manufacturing and supply of chocolate-based products for consumption; (5) the distribution of chocolate-based products for consumption.

Purchases and sales

Due to an erosion of margins, there has been a trend towards integrating sale and processing activities. ADM entered the processing sector by acquiring the global leader Grace Cocoa for instance. In fact, firms specialised in sales have become fewer, bigger, more diversified and better integrated vertically with producers (upstream) and the transport and processing companies (downstream).

▶

Cocoa processing

Ten firms are responsible for two-thirds of cacao-moulding activities, a market controlled by ADM, Cargill and Barry-Callebaut. These trends were boosted by the search for economies of scale (moulding being a capital-intensive activity), scope (progress in terms of research and development and logistics) and the presence of agglomeration externalities (physical proximity between the processing firms and the chocolate manufacturers). These three elements enhance the competitiveness of large firms.

Industrial chocolate

There are two types of companies present in this market: the big brands (Nestlé, Mars, Hershey, etc.) and the suppliers specialised in processing (ADM, Cargill, Barry-Callebaut, Bloomer). These four large suppliers account for 75 per cent of the industrial chocolate market. It should be pointed out, however, that the quantities of industrial chocolate supplied within integrated groups are higher than those placed on the market.

Consumption chocolate

Nestlé, Ferrero, Mars, Kraft Jacobs Suchard and Cadbury Schweppes control 50 per cent of the consumption chocolate market in Europe.

Distribution

In OECD countries, it is estimated that supermarkets account for 75 to 85 per cent of the food product distribution market. In France, supermarkets account for 78 per cent of the distribution market for consumption chocolate. It would seem that 'value' has shifted from upstream and the middle of the chain (producers and processing industries) to downstream. Although the price of industrial chocolate tends to decrease, this is not passed on to the retail price. This highlights the growing power of big brands and distribution channels. Generally, the share of producers as a percentage of the retail prices has steadily declined. Between 1996 and 2005, it ranged between 4 and 6 per cent for four African cocoa producing countries (Cameroon, Côte d'Ivoire, Ghana and Nigeria).

Source: UNCTAD (2008b).

At this stage, a key concept in the GVC analysis is that of 'governance'. It refers to the relations between firms and those between firms and producers: What should be produced? When? How? This form of governance is made necessary by, inter alia, the growth of consumer demand for non-standard products and the trend towards a tightening of sanitary and phytosanitary regulation (Gereffi et al., 2005).

The increasing market power of intermediaries no doubt represents a new threat to producers in the South, whose negotiating power is at risk of being considerably weakened. On average, it is estimated that coffee producers only receive 10 per cent of the value added linked to the sale of coffee-based products, compared with 20 to 30 per cent respectively for processing industries and distribution channels. The situation is the same for cocoa: producers only receive 15 per cent of the sale value for cocoa-based finished products. However, the most striking example is that of banana plantations: they only receive around 10 per cent of total sales, while the share of distribution channels can be as high as 40 per cent. Yet, banana is a quasi-finished product that requires very little industrial processing (FAO, 2007: 1).

Unequal ecological exchange

The logic of unequal exchange cannot be summed up solely in terms of declining export returns for countries of the South. According to ecological economics, the non-observance by market prices of the scarce and sometimes non-renewable nature of environmental resources is the cornerstone of a new form of unequal exchange between North and South. Indeed, according to this approach, the environmental 'energy' which is embedded in developing countries' exports is not factored into the invoicing of the prices they receive (see, for example, Howell, 2007; Muradian and Martinez-Alier, 2001). For instance, the massive exports of beef from Brazil to Europe and the United States have contributed to the deforestation of the Amazonian forest. Yet market prices do not take into account the ecological costs induced by this 'hamburger connection' (see Box 1.3). Hence the phrase 'environmental *dumping*', to refer to the fact that countries of the South sell at a price that does not include any form of compensation for the various forms of degradation (soil erosion, water and air pollution, climate change, etc.) as well as the depletion (deforestation, loss of biodiversity, etc.) of their environmental resources.

According to ecological economics, countries of the North are dependent upon the export of 'biocapacity' by countries of the South because of their overconsumption model. Biocapacity is defined by the Global Footprint Network (GFN) as the 'biologically productive area actually available [in a given country]: crop land, fisheries, forests, etc.' In contrast, the concept of 'ecological footprint' assesses 'the pressure exerted by populations on the Earth. It measures the biologically productive surface of land or sea required to provide the resources consumed by countries and to absorb the waste they produce.' Biocapacity and the

---

Box 1.3 'The hamburger connection'

In the 1980s, the environmentalist Norman Myers (1981) coined the phrase 'the hamburger connection' to show the link between the export of beef from Central American countries to the United States and deforestation. Brazil is without a doubt the most convincing example of this phenomenon.

Between 1990 and 2000, the total cleared areas in the Brazilian Amazonian forest grew from 41.5 million hectares to 58.7 million hectares; these lost surfaces are almost twice as large as Portugal. This ongoing deforestation is a consequence of the growing international demand for beef from Brazil. The devaluation of the Brazilian currency, the fact that the country was spared from some bovine diseases (mad cow disease, for instance) and that it offers sanitary and phytosanitary guarantees are the main factors behind the growth in meat exports from Brazil. Between 1990 and 2002, bovine livestock more than doubled in Brazil, growing from 26 million to 57 million. In turn, this increased the loss of arable land to make way for grazing land. The increase in the size of pasture land is a cause of deforestation – a phenomenon that accentuates climate change – as 80 per cent of new cattle graze in the Amazonian forest (Demaze, 2008; Kaimowitz et al., 2004).

---

ecological footprint are measured in global hectares (gha). A country is 'in debit' when its ecological footprint is higher than its biocapacity – it consumes more environmental resources than it has; while it is 'in credit' when its biocapacity is higher than its ecological footprint – it consumes fewer environmental resources than it has.

According to GFN (2010), every inhabitant on the planet consumed 2.6 gha on average in 2007, while only having 1.8 gha of biocapacity (see Figure 1.7). This growing ecological deficit is a corollary of the overconsumption model of countries of the North. Still according to the GFN, if all inhabitants of the world adopted the same style of living as an average American, we would need the resources of five planets such as ours. Indeed, average Americans consume twice the environmental resources they have. Unfortunately, we only have one Earth!

In spite of their big ecological footprint, countries of the North preserve their biocapacity better than countries of the South: they are confronted with less deforestation, water pollution, greenhouse gas emissions, etc. (see Figure 1.8). How can we explain this paradox? According to ecological economics, countries of the North have transferred the ecological costs linked to their mode of consumption to countries of the South (Jorgenson and Rice, 2005). For example, between 1976 and 1997, the European Union imported three to five times more 'pollution-intensive' goods – whose production generates huge levels of pollution – than it exported

(Schütz et al., 2004: 40). This degradation of the environment in the South is heightened by the decline in the price of primary products, the unfair competition by countries of the North and the recurring economic crises.

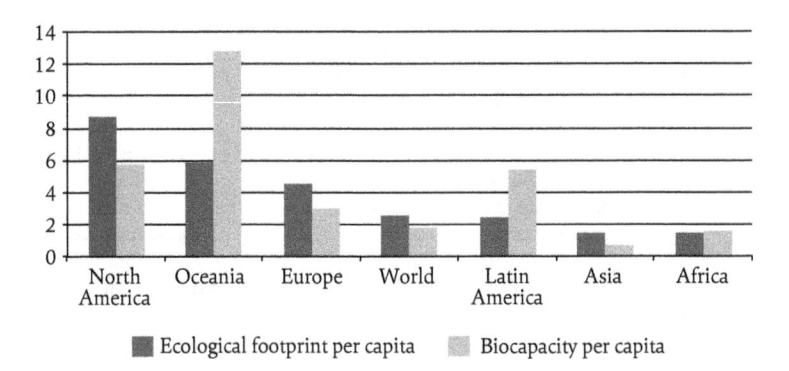

Figure 1.7   Ecological footprint and biocapacity in 2006 (in gha)

Source: GFN (2010).

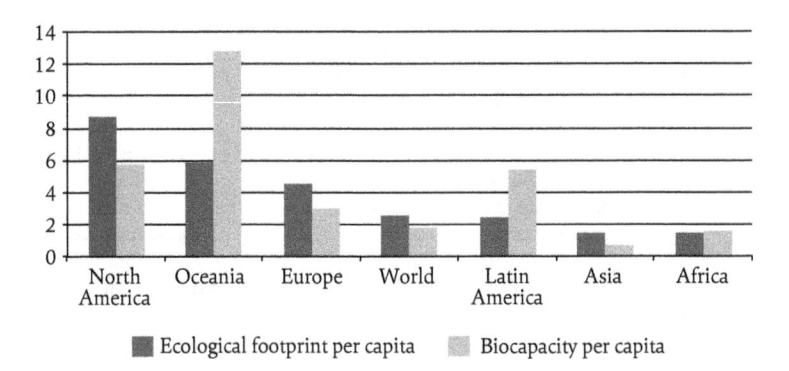

Figure 1.8   Changes in ecological footprint and biocapacity 1961–2006 (%)

Source: GFN (2010).

The judgement of ecological economics is therefore final: the consumption model in the North is not sustainable. It is based on taking over the biocapacity of the South and transferring the environmental costs to the South. This unequal ecological exchange is prompted by inequalities between nations, those between consumers of the North and producers of the South and those internal to countries of the South (Howell, 2007; Muradian and Martinez-Alier, 2001).

In summary, from the point of view of its effects, international trade has not been the desired tool for economic catch-up: over the last few decades it has failed to take into account the economic, social and environmental concerns of the poorest countries of the planet. Neither has it been fair in terms of the processes it implemented. As we shall see, this unequal exchange is the outcome of biased practices and asymmetric rules that – it is well known – disadvantage developing countries. This is precisely what makes international trade particularly unfair in the eyes of many observers.

Biased Practices...

Contrary to the myths disseminated by the 'official history of capitalism' (Chang, 2002, 2008), the rules of international trade have always been asymmetrical. To develop on the economic level, rich countries used to resort to selective and strategic industrial and trade policies. They protected their infant industries through prohibitive tariffs until the latter became competitive on the international scene. If Britain became the *leading* economy in the nineteenth century, it is, among other reasons, because it maintained high tariffs more than half a century after the Industrial Revolution. The United States followed the same path between 1791 and 1846, then between 1860 and 1945. This is why Paul Bairoch (1995 [1993]: 32) said that this is 'the mother country and bastion of modern protectionism'. Similarly, the historian and economist Ha-Joon Chang argued that American industries received the highest level of protection in the world between 1870 and 1945. Britain was therefore the first nation to successfully implement an aggressive strategy for the promotion of infant industries, while the United States remains the fiercest proponent of this strategy (Chang, 2002).

Once their industrial superiority became immune to any serious international competition, developed nations started praising the virtues of free trade for strategic reasons: on the one hand, their industries no longer needed protection and, on the other, they had to open up new markets, which required that trade barriers be reduced abroad. In other words, developed nations started preaching to the rest of the world the opposite of what made them successful; this mystification was denounced at the time by Friedrich List (1885 [1841]), one of the most prominent advocates of the argument for the protection of infant industries, following in the footsteps of supporters of the *American System*, such as Alexander Hamilton (Chang, 2002; Magnusson, 2004).

Through this ideological discourse and the way it was implemented in the colonies, rich nations limited the chances of developing countries applying the same methods that had enabled their industrialisation. Britain, for instance, delayed the industrial development of its former colonies by (1) subsidising the export of primary products and removing customs duties that Britain applied to these products; (2) prohibiting high value added manufacturing activities by law; and (3) discouraging exports that competed with those of Britain (Chang, 2002). It is precisely this imperialism that plunged most former colonies into the 'trap' of specialisation in primary goods, which often translated into a turn away from subsistence crops and towards cash crops. These countries will have learnt this historical truth of international trade at their expense, namely that 'those who don't obey the rules win' (Bairoch, 1995 [1993]:168).

In the twenty-first century, these practices prevail, in part thanks to the manipulation by rich countries of the rules that regulate international trade. Indeed, the gap between the reality of their industrial and trade policies and their free market rhetoric is still just as wide and harmful to the poorest countries.

Selective liberalisation and tariff escalation

The reduction of customs tariffs has always been included on the agenda of multilateral negotiations. In the long term, they have certainly been lowered to a great extent, which has enabled the expansion of international trade. But for developing countries in particular, this decrease went together with the introduction of a set of non-tariff barriers whose effect has also been to distort trade exchanges. 'Non-tariff barriers' refers to a set of measures such as quantitative restrictions (quotas for example), sanitary and phytosanitary standards, quality standards, administrative and customs procedures, non-tariff charges, etc. While some of these are justified by legitimate concerns (for example sanitary and phytosanitary standards), others may be motivated by protectionist concerns (for example, restrictions linked to 'rules of origin'). In order to limit their use, the World Trade Organization (WTO) recommends that these non-tariff barriers be converted into customs tariffs that provide an equivalent level of protection. This process, called 'tarification', has led to the following paradox: countries that agreed to lower their tariff barriers sometimes ended up with higher tariffs than those used before the agreements on the reduction of tariffs (Stiglitz and Charlton, 2005: 49–50).

In order to encourage developing countries to access their market, rich countries set up preferential agreements. Some of those are included in the multilateral framework of the Generalised System of Preferences, while others apply to specific regions or groups. In the latter case, we can mention for instance the United States' African Growth and Opportunity Act (AGOA) or the European Union's Everything but Arms (EBA) programme. These preferential agreements enable LDCs to export a broad range of products to rich countries under conditions that are more advantageous in principle. Due to their selective nature, however, these remain rather ineffective. Japan, for instance, opens up its borders to 98 per cent of products, but excludes rice, sugar, fish and shoes. Likewise, AGOA excludes milk products, tobacco, ground nuts and sugar (Elliott, 2010).

When products exported by LDCs are covered by these preferential agreements, they can be subjected to quotas or restrictions pertaining to 'rules of origin'. This last phrase means that products arriving at the borders of rich countries must contain inputs that were 'significantly processed' in the LDCs. This eligibility criterion essentially aims to identify the origin of the product. But it also enables destination countries to collect trade statistics and take trade policy measures. At a time when increased commercial integration goes hand in hand with a disintegration of production processes (Feenstra, 1998), it goes without saying that this type of measure is a complex one to implement, both for destination countries and for beneficiary countries. For instance, the European Union EBA programme is in principle open to all products exported by LDCs. However, it includes a 'complex and opaque' rules-of-origin system which, in practice, heavily penalises the export of agricultural products, clothing and textile products that are labour-intensive (Elliott, 2010).

The problem is that regional and bilateral preferential agreements – whose estimated number is more than 300 – are distinguished by their product coverage rate, whether they are free of quotas or tariffs, their duration and the flexibility of their rules of origin. This opacity/complexity, described by the expression 'spaghetti bowl', has generated heated debates that have focused on, among other issues, the impact of the 'erosion' of trade preferences. The economist Jagdish Bhagwati, renowned for his extreme views in favour of laissez-faire, does not hesitate to speak of the 'termites' that undermine the basis of multilateral trade (Bhagwati, 2008).

This form of selective liberalisation reduces not only the volume and the value of exports from developing countries, it also impacts their *composition*. For example, customs duties imposed by developed countries on processed agricultural products are much higher than for basic agricultural products. The tariffs applied by Canada, Japan and the European Union on basic food products are respectively 3, 35 and 15 per cent, against 42, 65 and 24 per cent when they have reached their last phase of transformation (Stiglitz and Charlton, 2005: 51; World Bank, 2002).

This tariff escalation (in other words, tariffs are higher at each level of processing of primary agricultural products) contributes to reducing market shares for developing countries in the global trade of processed agricultural products and to discourage their industrialisation in high value added sectors. Between 1981 and 1991, and 1991 to 2000, the share of processed agricultural products in agricultural trade rose from 60 to 66 per cent. In the meantime, the share of developing countries in this market decreased from 27 to 25 per cent; for LDCs, this share dropped from 0.7 to 0.3 per cent (FAO, 2004: 26).

Agricultural dumping and support to producers

The subsidies enjoyed by farmers in developed countries represent without a doubt the most highly publicised and most controversial trade policy tool. By subsidising agricultural exports, developed countries resort to *dumping*: they export their products at prices lower than domestic ones. Although the use of such instruments is regulated by the WTO, there remains a great degree of opacity.[3]

Contrary to general opinion, it would seem that the impact of these subsidies on international trade is generally less important than that of tariff barriers for example (Hoekman et al., 2004). Besides, they do not seem to represent the most significant part of the Producer Support Estimate (PSE). This indicator was developed by the OECD in order to measure agricultural support policies. It adds up the monetary value of three types of measurements: budgetary transfers to producers, market price support measures and tax benefits (see Box 1.4).

In the period 1986–8, the PSE amounted on average in the OECD countries to 37 per cent of gross farm receipts. In 2007–9, it was on average 22 per cent, the maximum and the minimum being recorded respectively in Norway (60 per cent) and New Zealand (less than 1 per cent). In spite of this drop, support to agricultural producers remains very high (OECD, 2010). To put it into perspective, the $252 billion allocated to producers in 2007–9 represents more than twice the amount of official development assistance.[4] To justify and legitimise this support, the argument generally bandied about is that of the protection of small farmers and rural livelihoods. In reality, the richest producers are the ones mostly benefiting from it. According to the WTO (2003: 21), the top 25 per cent of the richest producers in the European Union, the United States, Canada and Japan receive respectively 70, 89, 75 and 68 per cent of the total agricultural subsidies.

Box 1.4 Definition of the Producer Support Estimate

The PSE is a concept that was popularised by the OECD at the end of the 1990s. It measures the annual monetary value of gross transfers from consumers and taxpayers to agricultural producers, measured at the farm-gate level, arising from policy measures that support agriculture, regardless of their nature, objectives or impacts on farm production or income. The PSE adds together the monetary value of three types of measurements.

Budgetary transfers: 'Policy measures that provide payments to farmers based on criteria such as the quantity of a commodity produced, the amounts of inputs used, the number of animals kept, the area farmed, or the revenue or income received by farmers; payments to inputs suppliers to compensate them for charging lower prices to farmers; or to subsidise the provision of on-farm services.'

Market price support: 'Policy measures that maintain domestic prices for farm commodities at levels higher (or occasionally lower) than those at the country's border.'

Revenue forgone: 'Policy measures that provide implicit transfers through tax concessions or fee reductions that lower farm input costs (for example, for credit, energy and water).'

These transfers are measured as gross figures, without taking into account the adjustments that producers may make to receive the support, in other words to fulfil the conditions necessary to access the payment.

For comparative purposes, it is however preferable to measure the PSE in relative terms (as a percentage of gross farm receipts) as this is a nominal measure influenced by inflation and the evolution of exchange rates.

Source: OECD (2009).

From the point of view of developing countries, the protection thus given to farmers is a symbol of the blatant inequalities of international trade and the hypocrisy of developed countries. Indeed, it contributes to the depreciation of the prices of main agricultural products exported by developing countries, the reduction of their export revenue, the lowering of their market shares and *in fine* the depriving of a large part of the global workforce of opportunities for a decent income (Diao et al., 2003). As an example, according to Oxfam (2004), the support given by OECD countries to their cotton producers causes an annual loss of $250 million to 10 million producers earning a living from cotton in West and Central Africa.

Combined effect of the various trade policies

Overall, the obvious protectionism of developed countries can be summed up as follows:

- primary products not produced by the North are lightly taxed (such as cocoa, coffee, etc.); however, tariff escalation applies at each phase of their processing;
- primary products for which the North competes with the South (cotton, sugar, rice, etc.) are generally subsidised and/or submitted to tariff peaks;
- manufactured products for which the South has a comparative advantage face tariff and non-tariff barriers (quotas, restrictions on rules of origin, etc.).

In order to measure the combined impact of the distortions induced by these various trade policies, a number of indicators were developed, such as OTRI (Overall Trade Restrictiveness Index) and MA-OTRI (Market Access Overall Trade Restrictiveness Index). Four lessons can be learnt from estimates given on these in the *Global Monitoring Report* (World Bank and IMF, 2008, 2009).

First, the levels of trade protection remain relatively high everywhere in spite of a downward trend. As a general rule, agricultural products are more heavily taxed than manufactured products. Second, non-tariff barriers have a more restrictive effect on trade than customs tariffs. Third, tariff and non-tariff barriers remain high on products for which LDCs have a comparative advantage. For instance, OECD countries hold the record for the highest protection level for agricultural products in the world. The uniform tariff they apply to imported agricultural products was estimated on average at 43 per cent in 2006. However, for products such as cereals, the level of protection is simply unbelievable (into three figures). Finally, the result of all this is that trade barriers are less important in the framework of North–North trade than in North–South trade. For example, the United States collects more taxes on products coming from Bangladesh and Cambodia than on those from England and France (Progressive Policy Institute, 2002).

... Facilitated by Asymmetric Game Rules

According to Joseph Stiglitz and Andrew Charlton (2005: 82), international trade turned out not to be the redistribution tool hoped for due to a deficit in 'procedural fairness'. This notion 'focuses on the openness and transparency of the negotiation process, and the manner in which the discussions are conducted'. It can be addressed from several perspectives: the setting of the global negotiation agenda, the taking into account of initial conditions, the settlement of disputes, the imposing of sanctions and the broadening of WTO powers.

Although agreements negotiated at the WTO are based on a principle of consensus – unlike in other institutions such as the IMF and the World Bank – this has not led, according to Stiglitz and Charlton, to a better management of the needs of developing countries, especially the poorest of them. From their point of view, the agenda of the rounds of multilateral negotiations that have taken place since the creation of the General Agreement on Tariffs and Trade (GATT) in 1947 (replaced by the WTO in 1995) was determined on the basis of the interests and priorities of rich countries: advances were made on the items relevant to them (intellectual property rights, the liberalisation of financial services, the liberalisation of imports in developing countries) and not on those that could have generated more profit for developing countries (the elimination of subsidies and tariffs on their main exports, namely agricultural products and textiles; the liberalisation of labour-intensive services).

Beyond the biased nature of the multilateral negotiations agenda, the neglect of initial conditions is also problematic, according to Stiglitz and Charlton. Let us take the case of the liberalisation of imports in the case of developing countries. It is often boosted following multilateral and bilateral negotiations. It is sometimes imposed on a unilateral basis and without any compensation from International Financial Institutions, namely as part of economic recovery programmes. But generally speaking, it must be noted that this is a measure that serves the interests of rich countries more than those of developing countries. First, it is a strategy that undermines the economic development prospects in the South. Tariff protection not only generates fiscal revenue, but, as we have seen, it also protects infant industries. Second, the level of tariff protection currently observed in developing countries is rather low, given the differences in living standards. Without mentioning the *de facto* protection provided by transport costs, which were high at the time, the United States applied an average tariff of 40 per cent on imports in the nineteenth century, at a time when their GDP per capita represented three-quarters of that of Britain. In comparison with the average tariffs they apply today and the gap in living standards that separates them from rich countries, there is no doubt that developing countries are the real 'champions' of free trade (Chang, 2002). Thus, by encouraging developing countries to liberalise their imports, rich countries seem to have overlooked the impact that trade protection has had on their economic development. Finally, what is most 'unfair' is that while developing countries are increasingly pressurised to liberalise their imports, rich countries continue to maintain high barriers vis-à-vis developing countries' main exports. This 'double standards' approach, to quote a report by Oxfam (2002), is one of the basic tenets of the criticism made by movements aspiring to a fairer trade system.

Besides, at the level of dispute settlement, the WTO operates in a way that reflects power asymmetries between rich countries and developing countries. According to Chang (2008:37), trade negotiations at the WTO are 'like a war where some people fight with pistols while the others engage in aerial bombardment'. On the one hand, the financial and human costs linked to the lodging of complaints deter the poorest countries from resorting to the Dispute Settlement Body. Between 1995 and 2002, not a single complaint was lodged by a country ranked as LDC. However, one in two complaints was lodged by Japan, the United States and the European Commission (Stiglitz and Charlton, 2005: 83). On the other hand, the settlement of complaints is generally more favourable to rich countries. In their case, the rate of success has gone from 40 per cent under the GATT system to 74 per cent since the creation of the WTO. For developing countries, this indicator went from 36 to 50 per cent (Stiglitz and Charlton, 2005: 84).

These power asymmetries also show at the level of sanctions. If bilateral or multilateral agreements are violated, the sanction takes the shape of higher tariffs. However, this type of sanction has little impact in the majority of cases when it is imposed by a small country on a rich country. Besides, the small country often has little incentive to take such measures due to various forms of reprisal it might suffer in the future. On the other hand, when the big country erects new barriers as a response to a lack of reciprocity, the impact on the small country is considerable.

Finally, there is the growing political power of the WTO – which tends to cover an increasingly broad range of areas (intellectual property, competition policy, public procurement, etc.); these tend to congest the negotiation agenda and exclude developing countries that do not have the means to actively take part in all negotiation processes. According to Stiglitz and Charlton, this political 'space' must be tightly overseen, as they fear the WTO will otherwise overstep into issues of national sovereignty. From their point of view, the broadening of WTO powers must be restricted to issues around which collective action on a global scale is required, and for which benefits to developing countries are demonstrated.

Conclusion

In November 2009, citizens from all around the world gathered in Seattle in order to disrupt the multilateral negotiations led under the auspices of the WTO and to make their voices heard, as well as those of citizens disheartened by the government and market duet. According to many observers, these events marked the birth of alterglobalist movements. It would be a caricature to consider them as protectionists or antiglobalists. In fact, it is because everyone recognises the important function of global redistribution played by international trade that discussions on it can generate such levels of tension. Therefore, the issue cannot be addressed in such simplistic terms as free trade vs. protectionism, or as being for or against globalisation. The real questions are: what kind of international trade and what kind of globalisation? Alterglobalist movements want another globalisation, based on openness, where trade is a tool for development and where the concerns of mankind are not sacrificed on the altar of the logic of capital accumulation. 'Poverty in Plenty', to quote the title of a text by John Maynard Keynes (1973 [1934]) – such is the paradox of globalisation today. If mankind never had so much wealth as in this era, it also never had so many poor in all its history than in this same era of globalisation. It is therefore hardly surprising that some global actors have attempted to offer new alternatives in face of the devastating cynicism of the free market and the surrender of nation states to it. This fight for another globalisation is the stance adopted by many global social movements, among which Fair Trade can be included.

2

The Fair Trade Universe

The old imperialism – exploitation for foreign profit – has no place in our plans. What we envisage is a program of development based on the concepts of democratic fair-dealing. [...] Only by helping the least fortunate of its members to help themselves can the human family achieve the decent, satisfying life that is the right of all people. (Harry S. Truman, Inaugural Address, 20 January 1949, quoted in Rist, 2006 [1996]: 71–2)

Since Truman inaugurated the era of development, the fight for fairer and more balanced North–South relations was led by an ever-growing number of actors around the world. Within this global movement, which today promotes the idea of another form of globalisation, Fair Trade appeared as a specific response to the development challenge in the South. It refers to a form of solidarity approach that aims to ensure a decent income for producers and workers of the South in the framework of the trading relations they maintain either directly or indirectly with economic actors based in the North:

> Fair trade is a trading partnership, based on dialogue, transparency, and respect, that seeks greater equity in international trade. It contributes to sustainable development by offering better trading conditions to, and securing the rights of, marginalized producers and workers – especially in the South. Fair trade organizations, backed by consumers, are engaged actively in supporting producers, awareness raising and in campaigning for changes in the rules and practice of conventional international trade. (Definition of Fair Trade by the FINE Platform)[1]

To some extent, this definition can be considered a common denominator for many actors of the movement. If its goals generate relative consensus, we must nevertheless recognise that Fair Trade suffers deep wounds caused by the antagonistic directions that its protagonists want the movement to follow.

A Brief History of the Movement

According to most existing research works, the history of Fair Trade started just after the Second World War. It was initially a *solidarity approach*, referred to in those days as *solidarity trade*. In the middle of the 1960s, a new *protest movement* saw the light of day. It aimed to introduce *alternative trade*. A few decades later, the concept of Fair Trade has gained strength. It is based on an 'ethical label' promoted by actors from the associative movement.

From solidarity trade to alternative trade

Initiatives on the selective purchases of products from poor countries began to multiply following the end of the Second World War. They share three main characteristics. First, they were led by religious movements. Second, the promotion of a fairer North–South trade was later attached as a new component of a solidarity approach thus far confined to specific causes and social groups (namely, the cause of refugees and other war victims). Finally, based initially on a charity principle, these initiatives did not aim to express dissent against the established order, they simply hoped to alleviate its harmful consequences. This approach was in keeping with the times as illustrated in the preceding extract from Truman's Inaugural Address.

In North America, two Mennonite organisations were the precursors of solidarity trade: Ten Thousand Villages (TTV, previously Mennonite Central Committee Self Help Crafts) and SERRV International (Sales Exchange for Refugee Rehabilitation and Vocation). TTV's involvement in solidarity trade started in 1946 with the journey made by the business woman Edna Ruth Bieler to Puerto Rico. She was especially struck by the great poverty suffered by craftswomen. Under her impetus, TTV started importing textile products made in Puerto Rico and Jordan in order to resell them within a network of Mennonite churches and women's groups in the United States. In 1950, TTV set up a project to provide assistance to Palestinian refugees in Jordan. This project was renamed SELFHELP Crafts in 1968 and led to the inauguration in 1972 of the first SELFHELP shop in the United States. At the end of the 1980s, the number of

SELFHELP shops in the United States and Canada was estimated at more than 120 (Fridell, 2007). In 2006, TTV reached a record $20 million in sales (see its website).

SERRV initially purchased handicrafts (including watches) made by refugees in Europe in order to resell them in the United States. As of the 1950s, SERRV focused its action on crafts artists living in the South. Its action became more and more popular thanks to its partnership with the Church World Services. In 2008, its annual sales were estimated at close to $10 million (see its website).

In Europe, the British NGO Oxfam was one of the pioneers of the movement for solidarity trade. Originally, its mission was to collect funds in order to help war victims confronted by famine. At the end of the war, it set itself the mission of fighting poverty in the South. From 1950, it started selling handicrafts made by Chinese refugees. In 1964, the first alternative trade organisation (Alternative Trade Organization) was created. In parallel, in continental Europe, SOS Wereldhandel, later renamed Fair Trade Organisatie, was founded in 1959 in the town of Kerkrade (Netherlands) by a group of young members of the Catholic party. This association initially supported poor communities in the south of Europe by providing vocational training. In 1967, it started specialising in the import of products from the South. In 1969, it opened the first World Shop. Initially specialised in the sale of handicrafts and cane sugar, World Shops gradually broadened their product range. The introduction of coffee in 1973 marked the gradual substitution of handicrafts with agricultural products (Fridell, 2007).

Some authors argued that Abbé Pierre's plea of 1971 to help Bangladesh, a country gripped in the throes of the political split with Pakistan at the time, initiated the Fair Trade approach in France. His idea of twinning communes in France with communes in Bangladesh led in 1972 to the creation of the UCOJUCO (Union des Comités de Jumelage de Coopération; Union of Cooperation Twinning Committees) whose mission was initially to collect funds for the communes of Bangladesh. Two years later, Artisans du monde was founded by UCOJUCO in order to promote handicrafts from the South. In 1975, Artisans du monde and UCOJUCO split following divergences on the direction of their movement (Ballet and Carimentrand, 2007; Jacquiau, 2006).

While initially following a solidarity trade approach, these movements later significantly evolved in terms of their theoretical and ideological tenets. In the 1960s, with the growing influence of Third Worldism, the problems faced by countries of the South as well as the solutions that should be provided to them were conceptualised in a manner that departed from the prevailing ideas thus far. In those days, the heterodox economic theories embodied by the structuralist school of thought and dependency theory had started to wield considerable intellectual influence in Third Worldist spheres. Structuralist economists of Latin America, those of the Economic Commission for Latin America (ECLA) especially, attempted to highlight the mechanisms of unequal exchange between the *centre* of the capitalist system and the *periphery*, namely the age-old declining terms of trade for primary products exported by the periphery in comparison with the manufactured products it imported from the centre.

In order to pull out of underdevelopment, they urged countries of the periphery to adopt industrialisation strategies based on import substitution. In other words, these countries should promote industrial development via the domestic production of items that were previously imported. This requires tariff protection for the infant industries as well as exchange policies through which technologies and intermediary goods necessary for the industrialisation process would be imported at little cost (Oman and Wignaraja, 1991).

Although it included several currents within it, dependency theory generally had a pessimistic outlook with regard to capitalism. In the same vein as structuralist economists, advocates of dependency theory see international trade as a major mechanism whereby the periphery is exploited by the centre. However, from their point of view, the import substitution strategies, as advocated by structuralists, contribute to increasing the dependency of the periphery instead of emancipating it. On the one hand, they cause the industrialisation of the periphery to be more dependent upon the import of technology and intermediary goods from the centre. On the other, the specialisation in the export of primary products tends to remain unchanged due to the need to finance the imports made necessary by the industrialisation process. Based on this logic, authors such as André Gunder Frank ruled out the very possibility of a capitalist development of the periphery. According to him, development and underdevelopment are the 'two sides of the same coin', as development in the centre of the capitalist system is based on maintaining underdevelopment in the periphery. Thus, to come out of underdevelopment, it has been suggested that the periphery should disconnect itself from the global capitalist economy, or even that it should launch into a socialist revolution (Oman and Wignaraja, 1991).

The slogan 'Trade not Aid' was launched in this context in 1964, at the first United Nations Conference on Trade and Development (UNCTAD), an institution whose first Secretary was actually the Argentinian structuralist economist Raúl Prebisch. The agenda of the Third Worldist movement was henceforth to challenge the established order and campaign for a new world economic order in which the legitimate concerns of developing countries would be taken into account (Rist, 2006 [1996]).

In this context, solidarity trade organisations began to radicalise themselves and to structure their initiatives around 'alternative trade'. Religious charity was no longer a satisfactory response. From the first alternative trade organisation created by Oxfam in 1964 to the World Shops that appeared later, political activism gradually took over the charity approach. Their radical questioning of the free market approach was matched by the development of integrated value chains that operate outside of the system: products (initially handicrafts, then increasingly agricultural products) were imported from the South by group purchasing organisations to be sold in dedicated shops in the North. However, a major drawback of this approach is that it forces Fair Trade to remain a very small niche organisation, precisely because of its non-integration into standard sale and distribution channels.

The adventures of the Fairtrade label

As was the case in the genesis of solidarity trade, the religious influence was also present when the trade labelled 'Fair' was launched, fading out later on. In 1985, Frans van der Hoff, a Dutch priest who had been living in Mexico since 1973 and his fellow countryman Nico Roozen, who worked for the Solidaridad NGO, a Dutch ecumenical development aid organisation for Latin America, met in order to discuss the possibility of Indian producers living in the mountains of the south of Mexico to sell their coffee in the Netherlands under conditions that would enable them to protect their environment and live with dignity. They agreed on the fact that dedicated shops were not conducive to the development of the trade of 'ethical' products. They were both convinced that, in order to reach more consumers, 'ethical' products should enter the traditional sale and distribution channels. On this basis, they identified two options:

starting their own brand or creating a quality label (Roozen and van der Hoff, 2002: 9–13).

On this latter point, Nico Roozen suggested that the label be finally named Max Havelaar, after the title of Eduard Douwes Dekker's novel published in 1860 under the pen name of *Multatuli*, a Latin expression meaning 'I have greatly suffered'. This was far from a random choice. Max Havelaar was a civil servant in the colonial administration who, in the nineteenth century, spoke up against the many injustices suffered by producers on the island of Java (a former Dutch colony which is now part of Indonesia).

As their meeting ended, they agreed that Nico Roozen would be in charge of seeking markets in the Netherlands, while Frans van der Hoff would organise Indian producers and ensure the availability of a quality product. Upon his return, Nico Roozen met with roasting companies, including Douwe Egberts, which at the time controlled 70 per cent of the coffee market in the Netherlands, in order to sell them the idea of a coffee labelled 'Fair'. But his project met with little enthusiasm. The roasting companies had doubts as to the quality of the 'Fair' products and regarding uninterrupted delivery. They were not convinced that there would be a promising market for this type of product either. Besides, they did not want to 'introduce politics into supermarkets', as they feared a backlash from consumers.

After this first disappointment, Nico Roozen started thinking about launching a brand that would be traded by Solidaridad. But he quickly realised that this was not a feasible option, as the financial weight required was simply beyond their means. Ironically, it was by bluffing about the launch of a new coffee brand that Nico Roozen was able to generate new interest from the largest distribution chain – Albert Heijn – which preferred the idea of a label to that of a brand. After agreeing with Albert Heijn on the launch of Max Havelaar coffee and on a common charter, Nico Roozen was once again surprised by the defection of his partner only a few months before the crucial date. It should be said that, in the meantime, Douwe Egberts and Albert Heijn had colluded to kill the Max Havelaar coffee before it could be launched. But this was did not take into account the determination of the Solidaridad camp. In the end, the project of the coffee labelled 'Fair' was saved by small roasters and small distribution chains. On 15 November 1988 Max Havelaar coffee was introduced into supermarkets. The interest that it immediately generated among consumers quickly overcame the scepticism and dishonesty of Albert Heijn, which later started distributing Max Havelaar coffee (Roozen and van der Hoff 2002: 99–124).

The successful introduction of coffee in the Netherlands had a ripple effect in other European countries and in North America. After coffee, cocoa, tea, honey and bananas appeared in supermarkets under the Max Havelaar label. As was the case for coffee, the introduction of these products labelled 'Fair' into distribution channels met many obstacles. The two authors narrate the many cases of sabotage that they experienced when promoting the *oké* banana (detained ships, accidents at sea, give-away prices from competitors, etc.) (Roozen and van der Hoff, 2002).

Is Fairtrade innovative?

In the blurb for the book they co-wrote, Frans van der Hoff and Nico Roozen are described as being 'the authors of one of the most innovative initiatives of the economic world' (Roozen and van der Hoff, 2002). The interesting question is to what extent Fairtrade can be considered an innovative initiative.

Fairtrade was born out of a concern to level the balance in North–South relations. Indeed, its founders are convinced that (1) poverty in the South is an unacceptable condition that we must fight against; (2) we must move away from large-scale development projects, as they have not generally met the expectations of populations; (3) international aid creates passivity and dependency among beneficiary populations; and (4) North–South relations must be based on reciprocity (Roozen and van der Hoff, 2002). On second glance, these are the same ideas that the Third Worldist movement and alternative trade actors expressed under the slogan 'Trade not Aid'. So there is nothing new from this point of view.

Besides, given that the Fair Trade approach has existed since the end of the 1940s and that the value chains specialised in the sale of 'Fair' products started operating from the 1960s, it seems obvious that the 'innovative' nature of the approach initiated by the two founders is based first and foremost on the introduction of products labelled 'Fair' into traditional sale and distribution channels. I would argue that this labelling and standardisation approach is not as 'innovative' as all that. This does not mean, though, that I do not acknowledge the inherent merit of these two founders.

From the initial solidarity trade approaches to the launch of Max Havelaar coffee in 1988, close to 40 years went by. The question we might ask ourselves is why the labelling and standardisation approach took so long to appear. My personal answer is that the international context was not conducive to it. This approach could have been initiated by alternative channels, but this would have been incompatible with the ideology of their movement. Nico Roozen actually tells of the divergences he experienced with representatives of World Shops. These were in favour of launching a brand, but against the project of creating an ethical label. They had three main complaints in this respect. First, they felt that the distribution of products labelled 'Fair' via traditional channels would create unfavourable competition for them. Second, they could not envisage associating the actors of large distribution and the agrifood multinationals with the movement for a more balanced North–South trade. Finally, they feared that the sale of Fairtrade products on supermarket shelves would undermine the activist aspect associated to the spirit of their movement. As we shall see, these complaints are still valid today.

As much as the labelling/standardisation approach was unthinkable from an ideological point of view, it was equally difficult to envisage it from a practical point of view. In the North, distribution channels and the agrifood market had not yet reached the levels of horizontal concentration and vertical integration that they have today. In the South, in spite of the presence of intermediaries, agricultural value chains were strongly regulated by governments within the limits of national boundaries. International prices were not fully transmitted to producers due to, among others, existing price stabilisation mechanisms.

The emergence of the labelled approach at the end of the 1980s was certainly not driven by necessity. But a number of factors were conducive to it. From an ideological point of view, neoliberalism had become the dominant economic policy paradigm (see Box 2.1). It advocated the end of governmental regulation in the economic area and a return to the sacrosanct principles of the free market. In the South, the implementation of the tenets of neoliberalism in a context of economic crisis led to the withdrawal of the state from the agricultural value chains and to their liberalisation. This initially prompted an increase in the number of intermediaries. In the North, in the meantime, a twofold development took place. On one hand, distribution channels and agrifood industries had become increasingly oligopolistic. On the other, the degree of horizontal concentration increased along the agricultural value chains. On a global level, mechanisms regulating North–South trade were

Box 2.1 Neoliberalism

Neoliberalism is a political and economic doctrine that gained prominence in the wake of the Second World War with the creation of Mont Pelerin Society in 1947. Founded by the Austrian economist Friedrich Hayek, this organisation gathered together eminent personalities such as the economists Milton Friedman, George Stigler and Ludwig Von Mises, as well as the philosopher Karl Popper (Mirowski and Plehwe, 2009). The 'neoliberal' label is used to designate people, institutions or approaches that adhere both to the principle of individual liberties – namely entrepreneurial and trade freedom – as promoted by classical economic liberalism (hence the -liberal suffix) and to neoclassical economics – namely its blind faith in the virtues of the market economy (hence the neo- prefix). It would seem that the expression was first used at the end of the First World War by a group of economists and legal experts affiliated to the 'Freiburg school' and who wished to revive classical liberalism. It was later adopted in the 1970s by a group of economists from Latin America in order to promote a pro-market stance (Steger and Roy, 2010).

Neoliberalism postulates that the most effective and fairest way to advance society's welfare is to promote free enterprise and free trade. To this end, the state must guarantee the respect of individual liberties and private property rights. It should also ensure a smooth running of the market economy. For instance, it must not step in to set prices, impose tariffs or introduce other forms of distortions. The trio of deregulation, privatisation and promotion of a minimal social state is the de facto mode of 'governance' promoted by neoliberalism, which is also in favour of the isolation of central banks from any democratic pressure. According to its advocates, any other form of 'governance' would be inefficient for the economy and would threaten individual liberties.

After the end of the Second World War, Keynesianism was the dominant economic policy paradigm until the appearance of stagflation (stagnation + inflation) in the mid 1970s in most major economies of the developed world. This is when the 'neoliberal turn' started. Under the stewardship of Ronald Reagan and Margaret Thatcher, neoliberalism moved from the status of doctrine to that of economic policy programme: its keywords were market deregulation (the labour market and capital markets especially), privatisation of public enterprises and withdrawal of the 'welfare state'. The same principles were applied in developing countries in the framework of the 'conditionalities' attached to structural adjustment programmes conducted under the auspices of the World Bank and the IMF. This is when Margaret Thatcher uttered her notorious TINA: 'There Is No Alternative' to neoliberalism.

Neoliberalism had promised greater efficiency and more fairness. In reality, it mostly led to an increase of socioeconomic inequalities. According to David Harvey, the 'genius' of the neoliberal doctrine was to use words that we are deeply attached to (freedom, choice, rights, etc.) in order to hide its project of restoring/strengthening the power of dominating classes. To take the case of the United States, the 0.1 per cent richest people trebled their share of the national income between 1978 and 1999. This went up from 2 per cent to 6 per cent. The same trends can be observed in other OECD countries and in emerging countries, as well as China (Harvey, 2005; see also Duménil and Lévy, 2011).

gradually dismantled. The non-renewal in 1989 of the International Coffee Agreement is significant in this respect (Daviron and Ponte, 2005), alongside the disappearance of price stabilisation mechanisms, such as the Sysmin and the Stabex,[2] and the loss of importance that befell instruments such as the Common Fund for Commodities and the Compensatory Financial Facility of the IMF. The point made here is not that these mechanisms were efficient or that they actively worked in favour of developing countries. It is rather to demonstrate that Fair Trade took advantage of a relative institutional void to take over a global political space (Boris, 2005).

The labelled approach is therefore indeed the daughter of her time. Its innovative character, if we can describe it that way at all, resides in the fact that some actors were able to take a step ahead in a context where residual barriers were essentially of an ideological kind. Yet the dominant neoliberal discourse took no time to dismantle them. Frans van der Hoff and Nico Roozen actually stated that their approach was motivated by the desire to offer something concrete, as the time for protest seemed to have gone by. As we shall see, the emergence of the labelled approach created new opportunities for producers and workers of the South. At the same time, it created divisions within the Fair Trade movement, as well as causing the birth of competing initiatives whose ethical motivations remain to be clarified.

Two contrasting views of Fair Trade

There are roughly six categories of actors that operate within the Fair Trade universe. Upstream of the value chain, there are producer (or 'hired labour') organisations. Taking the legal form of an association or a cooperative is an important aspect, as it facilitates dialogue between producers and their many partners. It also enables a stronger development of associative life within communities at the grassroots level. But its main justification is mostly the need to make economies of scale. Given that the quantities produced by family farms taken individually are too small to be suitable for export, the adoption of an associative structure imposes itself in order to reach a certain scale of production and to encourage the sharing of best practices.

Downstream of the chain, we find the 'consum'actors' or 'ethical consumers'. The existence of this form of consumption in the North is the cornerstone of the system, as it provides an outlet to producers and workers in the South, who, under normal circumstances, would have had to face the tremors of the free market. In fact, the size of the market for Fair Trade products depends to a large extent on consumer willingness to pay.

There are four types of intermediaries in the middle of the chain: traders (importers/exporters), processing/manufacturing companies, trading/marketing companies and distribution networks. Labelling organisations are not outside the value chain *per se*. But it is more suitable to consider that they are active all along the value chain through their control, certification and licensing activities.

The relations between these different categories of actors depend on the type of 'governance'. Recent research tends to isolate two major approaches in the governance of Fair Trade value chains: the integrated model and the product certification model. It ought to be pointed out also that there exists a 'non-formal' Fair Trade sector that operates at the margins of the structures described above. These initiatives subscribe to the notion of a fairer trade between North and South, but according to criteria and modalities of their own.

The integrated model

This phrase refers to the value chains where economic intermediaries are specialised in the distribution and/or sale of 'Fair' products. This model corresponds to the alternative trade approach. The products – agricultural products or handicrafts – are purchased from producers in the South or by specialised group purchasing organisations in order to be sold in dedicated shops. To sell within the conditions of Fair Trade, producers of the South must conform to a clearly defined set of criteria.

At the global level, the World Fair Trade Organization (WFTO) federates specialised/alternative Fair Trade organisations. It has a regional office on each continent. At the European level, two major organisations operate on this type of value chain: EFTA (the European Fair Trade Association), which covers specialised importers from nine countries, and NEWS (the Network of European World Shops) which covers 2,500 World Shops distributed across 13 countries. In North America, the Fair Trade Foundation (FTF) brings together importers and distributors of Fair Trade goods.

In order to assert its specific position on the Fair Trade market, WFTO launched its own logo in 2004. Unlike the Max Havelaar label, which certifies products, the WFTO logo is only available to organisations that are '100 per cent fair'; in other words, those that (1) sell or buy products at Fair Trade conditions, (2) apply the principles of Fair Trade at all levels of their activity and (3) promote Fair Trade among suppliers and clients. The WFTO is currently developing a new Fair Trade-certified label based on the Sustainable Fair Trade Management System standard, which should enable a better treatment of the poorest producers, who are generally excluded by existing certification systems (crafts artists mainly).

Control all along the value chain is based on self-assessment. Members are generally required to fill in a questionnaire and, if applicable, to send requested documents to the WFTO monitoring department. After consideration, the latter provides its feedback in the form of recommendations and corrective measures. For these self-assessment reports to be approved, a minimum score should be obtained. The marks are provided by a third party.

Every year, the WFTO organises the World Fair Trade Day (on the second Saturday of May).

The product certification model

This model is embodied by the Max Havelaar/Fairtrade label (see below) and is literally based on the certification of products, unlike the previous approach that certifies organisations. The sale/distribution of certified products is in theory available to all corporations, provided that they comply with specific standards (namely generic standards; see below) and pay their annual licence fees to the label holder (namely the national labelling initiative). Unlike with the previous model, there is no requirement to be '100 per cent Fair Trade specialised' in order to obtain a licence for the sale or distribution of Fair Trade products. As a result, the classical sale and distribution channels can be more easily integrated.

In this model, producer organisations in the South that wish to sell their products under Fair Trade conditions must first of all obtain certification, which is subject to complying with the standards defined in this respect by the certification organisation. It is also important to point out that the label holder does not buy or sell any product. It rather trades the use of the said label.

Introduction to the Fairtrade System: The Role of FLO

The Fairtrade/Max Havelaar label is commercialised in consumer countries by 'labelling initiatives', which are not-for-profit associations (such as Max Havelaar France, Fairtrade Foundation in the United Kingdom, etc.). These are the linchpins of the system. At the national level, they ensure, among other things, coordination between the various actors and are responsible for marketing the label. Their resources are increasingly made up of licensing fees, and less and less from public subsidies. An important share is allocated to communication and awareness-raising costs. These labelling initiatives belong to what I describe as the 'protagonists' of Fairtrade, in opposition to 'supporters', a category that includes sympathisers, activists and other support movements.

At the international level, FLO is the federating entity whose mission is to promote the Fairtrade label. Created in Bonn (Germany) in 1997, FLO brings together 19 labelling initiatives covering 24 consumer countries, 3 Fairtrade marketing organisations, 3 international networks of producers and an associate member. In 2002, this NGO introduced the Fairtrade-certified label in order to increase its visibility on supermarket shelves and also to facilitate the trade of products bearing this label. Since then, national labels were gradually replaced. Only the United States and Canada kept their original label: Fair trade certified™. On this point, it is important to point out that FLO is especially concerned with distinguishing between the movement that it coordinates – Fairtrade, single word, no space between fair and trade – and the other movements that identify with the Fair Trade approach.

In terms of its structure, FLO is made up of two separate entities since 2004: FLO-ev, which defines the Fairtrade standards and supports producers, and FLO-cert, which is the certification entity. FLO is ISO 65-certified. The purpose of this certification is to ensure (1) the existence of a quality management system; (2) transparent processes; (3) the independence of the certification entity – namely FLO-cert – which is audited by a third party to assess its degree of compliance with the ISO 65[3] standard. FLO resources come from two sources (see the 2012 annual report): subsidies and donations (45 per cent) and membership fees (50 per cent).

With WFTO (previously IFAT, International Fair Trade Organization), NEWS and EFTA, FLO belongs to the FINE platform (acronym made up of the initials of each of these organisations) which is at the origin of the Fair Trade definition quoted above. The propaganda and sensitisation activities of these networks are coordinated by an advocacy office based in Brussels. They rely mostly on contributions from volunteers, whose number is estimated at more than 80,000 as far as Europe is concerned (Krier, 2008).

FLO is the cornerstone of the Fairtrade system. Its various activities can be split into four main categories. As a general rule, each of these functions falls under the responsibility of a specific department.

Sensitisation

For this model to be successful, it is crucial that FT products meet quality requirements and are accessible to consumers in the North. It is also important that the latter are sufficiently sensitised in order to shorten the 'distance' that separates them from the producers along the value chains. They must be informed of the conditions of production of most of the goods they consume as well as of the living conditions of those who produce them. This battle against the 'anonymity' of the market is one of the missions of labelling initiatives and of FLO, as it represents an unavoidable strategy in order to ensure consumers support the values of the movement and to build their trust. These sensitisation, promotion and marketing campaigns are also aimed at economic actors (large distributors, multinationals, etc.), the political class, international institutions, etc. In parallel, FLO and labelling initiatives conduct many 'networking' activities in order to find the partners that can help them in a support logic.

NGOs and development agencies sometimes help producers (by encouraging them to move towards certification) and labelling initiatives (through donations and sensitisation campaigns). Likewise, some organisations help producers that have received FT certification in their export procedures or in their search for working capital. Others are active in the system through research, documentation and the publication of documents on Fair Trade. Finally, labelling initiatives often work in partnership with organisations that promote labels that fall under the principles of sustainable development (for example Label-Step and Rugmark are labelling organisations specialising in international issues related to working conditions in the carpet industry).

Guaranteeing quality

One of the crucial aspects of FLO's work is to control quality and to guarantee both the quality and integrity of the Fairtrade label. Consumers want to feel reassured as to the quality of Fairtrade products. The traceability of Fairtrade products and the surplus consumers pay for them are also a concern. This component is managed by FLO-cert, which has a team of inspectors present all over the world. Two types of audit can be conducted: audits ahead of an initial request for certification (producers and hired labour organisations may want to obtain certification for some of their products; some intermediary organisations may apply to be licensed for sale/distribution purposes) and annual audits for the purpose of renewals. In both cases, the goal is to ensure that clients comply with FLO standards. As far as organisations of small producers are concerned, it ought to be pointed out that achieving certification is a relatively costly process (see Box 2.2).

Box 2.2   The cost of initial certification

The cost of initial certification is determined on the basis of the candidate's status: small producer organisations or hired labour organisations. Let us focus on the first case, which accounts for the bulk of the demand for certification. For initial certification, producer organisations are required to pay €525 in non-refundable processing fees. This is a one-time only payment.

Aside from processing fees, the cost of certification depends on four factors: the type of organisation (first, second or third grade), the number of members in the organisation (which determines the number of days required for inspection), the number of products to be certified, and whether a processing unit exists or not. For a first grade organisation, the basic cost of certification ranges between a minimum of €1,430 (less than 50 members) and a maximum of €3,470 (over 1,000 members).

If the organisation wishes to have additional products certified, it must pay a further €180 for each product. If it has a processing unit, charges range between a minimum of €210 (less than ten workers) and a maximum of €620 (over 100 workers).

For second and third grade organisations (small producer organisations affiliated to an organisation that has a central structure), the principles are the same. The central structure pays a basic rate of €1,530, to which are added certification costs for each organisation selected for the audit. The number of audited organisations is determined on the basis of the square root of the number of members, when this number is higher than 100. For example, if a third grade organisation has 256 members, only 16 of them will be audited.

The fees covering auditing costs are non-refundable – even in the event that certification is not granted. FLO-ev runs a certification fund to support producers, through which up to 75 per cent of the cost of certification can be covered.

An enigma remains however: the costs of certification are the same everywhere. Yet developing countries obviously do not have the same standard of living.

Source: http://www.flo-cert.net/flo-cert/65.html (rate applicable as of 1 January 2013; accessed in January 2013).

Organising and building the capacities of producers

In principle, developing countries are almost all eligible for the FT system. FLO is present mainly in three regions: Africa/Middle East; Asia; Latin America and the Caribbean. For each of these regions, a regional manager is appointed and backed by regional coordinators; these are present at the sub-regional level. Regional coordinators supervise the work conducted on the ground by liaison officers. These generally have a consultant status and represent FLO at the national level. Their mission is to support and mentor producers who wish to move towards certification – namely through training on the standards – as well as those who already hold their certification. Through the work of its liaison officers, FLO seeks to achieve economies of scale on coordination tasks, to strengthen the bargaining power of producer or hired labour organisations and to generate a complete uptake of FT principles.

Coordinating the movement

FLO coordinates the FT system through three main activities. First of all, it defines the standards, which are the overarching principles meant to regulate the conditions for the involvement of various actors within the Fairtrade system as well as the goals of the movement. An initial distinction can be made between generic standards and standards that apply to specific products. On this latter point, FLO chose not to certify handicrafts at this stage, as the adoption of the standards is considered difficult due to the broad diversity of production processes and costs. Certifiable products are for the most part agricultural (such as coffee, bananas, tea, etc.) and, to a lesser extent, horticultural (such as flowers and plants, fresh vegetables, etc.). In addition to those articles, FLO developed standards for sports balls, and recently even started certifying gold (more precisely 'gold and other related precious metals') in collaboration with the Alliance for Responsible Mining, a network of independent organisations. As for the certification of composite products (those for which a Fair Trade product is an important component), FLO requires that a *minimum of fair content* is defined, as the case may be, depending on the weight or liquid volume.

Generic standards can be divided into generic trade standards and generic standards applicable to producers. Generic trade standards apply both to producer organisations and traders. They are structured around five main aspects: (1) the payment of the *minimum guaranteed price* to producers; (2) the payment of the *development premium* which is managed by cooperatives or associations; (3) the provision of pre-financing facilities to producers who request them; (4) the signing of contracts that facilitate long-term planning as well as 'sustainable production'; (5) the guarantee of FT product traceability (both physical and administrative). It can be said that to a certain extent, these contracting terms are the identity cornerstone that helps distinguish the FT certification model from competing labelling approaches.

The generic standards applicable to producers are structured around four pillars: (1) economic development; (2) social development; (3) environmental development; (4) the respect of workers' rights. On this point, FLO distinguishes three types of standards based on the status of the certification applicant: the standards for small producers (see Box 2.3); the standards for 'contract production' (producers that are not yet legally structured as an organisation, but are temporarily sponsored by an NGO or a trader to help them access certification); standards for hired labour organisations.

These standards are not subject to the same timelines. FLO distinguishes between *entry or minimum requirements* (that need to be fulfilled before the issuance of certification) and *progress requirements* (which must be fulfilled within a specific period following successful certification). All these standards are defined by FLO-ev, which has a department specifically dedicated to this task. In contrast, operational criteria – or *compliance criteria* in FLO jargon – allow for the measurement and assessment of the fulfilment, or even the implementation, of these standards and are defined by FLO-cert. The list of compliance criteria is made available to inspectors and they use it as a roadmap.

The setting of FT prices and of the FT premium for the different certified products is another important part of FLO's coordination activity. The FT price calculated and defined by FLO is the minimum price guaranteed independently from market fluctuations. This is a price that is normally higher than the market price, as the production of FT products is more costly than that of conventional products. The FT price is a 'full price', as it includes the cost of 'sustainable production' (see Chapter 4).

Last but not least, the dissemination of information is a crucial component of FLO's activities. Given the large geographical scope covered, the increasing number of actors and the range of certified products, the flow of information is vital for the FT system to operate efficiently. Various stakeholders need to have access to up-to-date information for a

---

Box 2.3   The standards for small producers

Small producers are defined as producers for whom agriculture is the main activity and the main source of income. Family labour is supposed to be the main type of labour employed. Among small producers, FLO distinguishes between those whose products are labour-intensive (and often require the use of hired labour) and those whose products are not. In the former case, a number of additional criteria are taken into account. An association or cooperative of small producers must include at least 50 per cent of producers matching this definition. In their case, the standards are structured around four pillars.

Social development: Members must be small producers; they must promote democracy, participation and good governance among themselves; discrimination in any form must be prohibited.

Economic development: The FT premium must be managed in a transparent and collegial manner; it must be invested in promising sectors and must not be used for personal needs; producer organisations must aim to achieve better control along value chains.

Environmental development: The types of production (such as genetically modified organisms) and materials prohibited by FLO must not be used; an environmental committee must be set up; a set of measures must be taken regarding the management of the ground, water, fire, waste, etc. It should be pointed out that FT products are not necessarily cultivated according to the organic farming standards.

Respect for the rights of workers: FLO is party to most conventions of the ILO on the rights of workers; it prohibits child labour and forced labour; it advocates the freedom to join a trade union and the freedom from discrimination; the payment of the minimum wage, if possible, as well as some health and security regulations.

For each pillar, there are entry requirements (for instance, the prohibition of genetically modified organisms) and progress requirements (for instance, drafting a development plan in the 12 months following initial certification).

It should be pointed out that at the time of writing this book, FLO was in the process of drafting new standards, the New Standards Framework, as the existing model is considered complex and difficult to implement.

Source: http://www.fairtrade.net/standards.html; accessed in January 2013.

---

more efficient allocation of time and economic resources. FLO thus plays an important role of intermediation between the various protagonists. At the international level, it acts as an 'auctioneer' by connecting the supply and demand for FT products.

The Marketing Success of Fairtrade: Some Figures

In 2011, the Fairtrade logo was placed on products from 66 countries that were traded in a little more than 120 countries. The number of affiliated producer organisations rose from 508 in 2005 to 991 in 2011 (FLO, 2012), which is an average annual increase of around 14 per cent. Small producer organisations account for 73 per cent of this total against 25 per cent for hired labour organisations and 2 per cent for 'contract production' (FLO, 2011). In the coffee sector, 365 FT producer organisations are active (37 per cent of the total). Slightly fewer than 200 organisations received FT certification in the sector of 'agricultural fruits' (bananas, limes, cucumbers, mangos, pineapples, sweet peppers). Certification for tea and cocoa was granted to slightly fewer than 100 organisations for each product (Transfair USA, 2011).

Perceptions of the Fairtrade label

In 1997, a Eurobarometer survey on 'Fair' bananas showed that 71 per cent of the European population was unaware of the existence of Fair Trade products. Among those who were familiar with the issue, only 11 per cent had purchased a Fair Trade product (European Commission, 1997). Nowadays, this state of affairs seems long gone. Since then, thanks in part to the numerous sensitisation campaigns, the Fairtrade label has become increasingly well known. Likewise, the purchase of FT products continues to grow at enviable rates. According to a recent study commissioned by FLO and based on a sample of 17,000 people spread across 24 countries, 50 per cent of people are familiar with the Fairtrade label.[4] Beyond this, various opinion polls also showed that consumers are increasingly aware of the potential consequences of their consumption choices.

Sales

The spectacular growth in retail sales of products labelled 'Fair' is without a doubt the best indicator of their success. In 2004, these sales were estimated at €830 million. Seven years later, this figure had increased six-fold, reaching a record-breaking €4.9 billion. This is equivalent to an average annual growth of around 13 per cent for that period. This development explains the narrowing market shares of alternative trade organisations. According to a study funded by the Dutch World Shops Association, FT products accounted for 90 per cent of the value of Fair Trade product retail sales in 2007; the ratio must surely have increased since then. This 'success story', to quote the title of the publication, can be linked to the presence of FT products on the shelves of 112,000 supermarkets in Europe and North America (Krier, 2008). This relative monopoly incidentally justifies the focus placed by this work on Fairtrade. Broadly speaking, the share of Fairtrade in world trade remains marginal (see Chapter 5).

However, the Fairtrade market remains highly polarised. As a general rule, countries that have the most FT distributors – their number is estimated at 3,000 – are those with the highest turnover. The United Kingdom (30.4 per cent) and the United States (20.9 per cent) alone account for 51 per cent of the global market. In continental Europe, Germany (8.1 per cent), France (6.4 per cent) and Switzerland (5.4 per cent) have the largest FT markets (FLO, 2012).

The FT premium and its usage

In developing countries, the number of producers/workers involved in Fairtrade is estimated at between 1.2 million and 1.5 million. In 2011, producer organisations affiliated to the FT system received €65 million in premiums (FLO, 2012). The largest share of this premium was generally reinvested in building the production capacities of FT organisations (FLO, 2011).

The War of Labels

Fairtrade is the most widespread Fair Trade label today in the world.[5] Its success paved the way for new competitors seeking to challenge its monopoly as an 'ethical' label. Different actors lead this challenge: NGOs and non-profit-making organisations, large agrifood multinationals as well as giants of large-scale distribution. The following examples can be mentioned (see Ellis and Keane, 2008 for a more comprehensive review).

Let us start with FLO's major competitor, the American NGO Rainforest Alliance. Founded in 1987, its mission is to protect ecosystems and to preserve the biodiversity and sustainability of modes of production. It runs a sustainable agricultural programme whose first standards date back to 1991. These standards are not based on the organic farming specifications, but on those of the Sustainable Agriculture Network. The main certified products of Rainforest Alliance are coffee, cocoa, tea, flowers and fruits. It is criticised, however, on the grounds of: (1) failing to provide pre-financing facilities, (2) failing to guarantee a minimum price, (3) favouring plantations at the expense of family farms and (4) loosely granting the Rainforest Alliance label (a bag of coffee can be granted the Rainforest Alliance label if it contains 30 per cent of Rainforest Alliance -certified coffee).

UTZ Certified (formerly UTZ Kapeh) is the other major FLO competitor. Its mission is to improve the efficiency and market access of producers. It also aims to guarantee the delivery of quality products to consumers and corporations. It was created in 1997 by coffee producers from Guatemala and by the Dutch roaster Ahold Coffee Company. UTZ Kapeh means 'Good coffee' in Quiche (the Maya language). Its headquarters has been based in the Netherlands since 2002. Since 2007, the board chair has been Nico Roozen, the co-founder of Fairtrade. UTZ certifies coffee, cocoa, tea and palm oil. It offers real-time tracking of the agricultural products it certifies. It does not guarantee a minimum price. Prices are negotiated between sellers and buyers. According to this foundation, however, buyers are always prepared to agree a price increase which would reflect the value added provided by the label. The price of certification is also determined through a negotiation process between sellers and buyers. UTZ Certified does not interfere with the pricing mechanism. It simply levies administrative costs. However, it is criticised for having relatively loose standards on the environment and the rights of workers.

Founded in 1991 and based in Washington, the mission of the Smithsonian Migratory Bird Center is to study, popularise and protect migrating birds. It promotes a rather original label. In 1998, it introduced the Bird-friendly Coffee programme in order to promote practices that help protect the habitats of migratory birds. The coffee in question is a variety grown in the shade (as opposed to that grown in the sunlight) under the tree canopy. Organic certification is a prerequisite for obtaining this label. For the time being, its market is limited to Japan and the United States.

In France, Bio-partenaire (previously Bio-équitable), is an association founded in 2002 which unites small and medium enterprises in the organic agriculture sector and combines the organic farming approach with that of Fair Trade. Its set of specifications is based on a frame of reference certified by Ecocert, an organisation that specialises in organic certification. Bio-partenaire is present in many organic-fair value chains: cocoa, cotton, dried fruits, quinoa, argan, etc. Since 2006, with the support of the European Social Fund, it has set up the Bio-solidaire project, which aims to 'adapt the Fair Trade principles and criteria to so-called North–North trade, based on a universal Fair Trade logic' (see its website).

Among multinationals, Starbucks launched the CAFE programme (Coffee and Farmer Equity Practices) in 2008, which is audited by Scientific Certification Systems. The 'sustainability' criteria are structured around four components: the promotion of quality, economic accountability, social accountability and environmental leadership. According to its website, the purchases carried out by the multinational in accordance with these standards amounted to £299 million in 2009 against £39 million for purchases made under the Fairtrade label.

As far as distribution channels are concerned, the main threat to Fairtrade is the development of distributor brands. In France, for instance, we have the very telling example of the Leclerc chain of supermarkets. In addition to distributing FT products, Leclerc created Entr'aide, a range of products that follow Fair Trade principles on the basis of its own criteria. The objective is to offer a broad range of 'Fair' products at prices that are affordable for consumers. This desire to reduce the prices of 'Fair' products, however, is not seen in a positive light by many Fairtrade supporters (Karpyta, 2009: 72–81).

This proliferation of ethical labels triggered an all-out war between the main protagonists of what can only be described as the 'sustainable' market. To take the case of the United Kingdom, nearly 80 labels (ethical, environmental, organic) are identified among food products.[6] According to other sources, more than 600 labels exist in the United Kingdom alone.[7] There is no doubt that this proliferation of labels is an enormous headache for regulatory authorities.

In order to control the market of the sustainable or remain in it, three main approaches are deployed. First, the logic of legitimisation: the various protagonists all try to project themselves as builders of a sustainable world, either with the argument of a track record in this area – Leclerc supermarkets, for instance, claiming their status as 'pioneers of sustainable development' – or, in most cases, by positioning themselves as new advocates of a global cause that now document their practices and have some evidence to hand.

Second, there is a logic of differentiation: all try to insist on their specificities and on the reasons why they present the best approach. Fairtrade took care right from the start to stand apart from the historical Fair Trade/alternative approach, and its competitors followed suit, distancing themselves from the Fair Trade movement as a whole. UTZ Certified defines itself as a 'professional' organisation that wants to reassure consumers as to the quality and traceability of the products they buy. Unlike Fair Trade, it does not want to impose an additional price that consumers would certainly not want to pay. As for Rainforest Alliance, it considers its approach as motivated by a concern to develop knowledge and build production practices as well as the management capacities of producers. In contrast, it considers that Fairtrade focuses more on trading. Hence, it argues, their differences in terms of 'target' and 'strategy'. When Leclerc proclaims itself Fair Trade leader in France, it is also to stand apart from Fairtrade and lessen the latter's scope.

Finally, the logic of innovation: each organisation constantly attempts to innovate, not only to generate income but also to proactively meet the changing needs of multiple targets with different motivations. To this end, several strategies are employed: name changing (e.g. FLO, UTZ Certified), addressing an aspect that is insufficiently developed, or even overlooked, by competitors (e.g. Bird-friendly Coffee), creating economies of scope (e.g. Bio-équitable), loosening standards or reducing the cost of certification (e.g. the '30 per cent' of Rainforest Alliance), introducing technological innovations (e.g. UTZ Certified with its traceability system), broadening the range of products likely to be certified (e.g. FLO with gold), etc.

Conclusion

Initially borne by charitable motivations, the Fair Trade approach gradually became more radical from the middle of the 1960s. In the mid 1980s, under the influence of neoliberalism, this alternative trade project was amended and integrated into a reformist framework that no longer shies away from integrating the large distribution channels nor from working with the other great 'enemies' of yesteryear, the agrifood multinationals. But at the same time as this trade labelled 'Fair' started gaining popularity, new approaches appeared and challenged its hegemony, thus forcing it to drown in the broader but more competitive and uncertain market of the 'sustainable'. It seems that the founders of Fairtrade unwittingly opened a Pandora's box.

The fair and the sustainable are now ubiquitous. In terms of networks and activist support, we find 'Fair' towns, churches, synagogues, schools, universities, etc. As far as the products are concerned, the offer extended to tourism, art, the music industry, fashion, the 2012 London Olympics (where coffee, tea and chocolate, among other products, were 'Fair') and … intimate relationships. An English company – French Letter Condom

Company – recently started selling 'fair trade condoms', that are said to be less polluting and more environmentally friendly. On its website, it is said that this company is 'delighted' to have brought 'an ethical dimension to this fantastic new product'. 'Condom ethics' present the opportunity for making love with an eye on fair play![8] By inscribing itself within the perspective of the commodification of sustainability, which is itself an aspect of the 'commodification of everything' (processes, objects, social relations) (Fine and Leopold, 2002; Harvey, 2005), Fair Trade could not help but inspire strong controversy.

3

Controversies Around Fair Trade

hat is the impact of Fair Trade? Is it an effective measure in
the fight against poverty in the South? Is it an alternative to
neoliberal globalisation? These questions are not simple ones.
This is rightly so, as the debates on Fair Trade have oscillated between
the Scylla of superficiality and the Charybdis of dogmatism. Scientific
dogmatism is not necessarily a bad thing. The philosopher Karl Popper
even argued that a minimum of dogmatism is sometimes necessary in
order to protect scientific knowledge from the effects of new 'fashions'
and to measure the relevance of the theories we hold dear (Popper, 1970).
On the other hand, it becomes a reactionary position when it leads to
inhibiting self-criticism or the reappraisal of theoretical views held sacred
even when troubling 'facts' are presented as evidence.

Such dogmatism is present among some Fair Trade protagonists as
much as among their opponents. For the former, the nobility of their
mission and ideals is such that it cannot suffer any discordant tone or
objective evaluation that would reveal its limits. The substance of their
argument is as follows: 'Fair Trade works because it is meant to promote
social justice; many testimonies and clues – carefully selected, one might
add – demonstrate this; it cannot but work.' Conversely, for the latter, this
trade promotes a model that is questionable, as much from the point of
view of its moral inspiration as from that of its effectiveness. Its possible
achievements are kept quiet when they are not considered as 'anomalies',
with a limited life expectancy. In contrast, superficiality is based on the
current environment and on a selective take on 'what is being said, done,
seen or heard'. This is generally the position of an ill-advised public that
supports or opposes a cause in light of meagre information, thus becoming
more liable to media manipulation.

Beyond these positions, that relate more to an eristic than a heuristic approach, the debates around Fair Trade also tend to be flawed by amalgams between ideological presuppositions, theoretical formulations and empirical arguments (the 'facts'). On the question as to whether Fair Trade works, a neoliberal economist might answer in the negative, arguing that free trade is the only viable strategy (answer of principle) and that Fair Trade leads to overproduction (theoretical assumption). To further back this assumption, he might present a few hints and anecdotes collected here and there (empirical argument). On the other hand, a Fair Trade protagonist would argue that neoliberalism was not invented with the poor in mind (answer of principle), and illustrating this with carefully selected works (empirical argument), he would say that the movement he belongs to generates significant benefits for the South (theoretical assumption). Due to the scarcity of thorough empirical evaluations, among other things, it is not surprising that the debates around Fair Trade focus more on the ideological and theoretical aspects.

In any case, it is important to go through each of these analytical levels (ideological presuppositions, theoretical formulations, empirical arguments), which are relatively autonomous from one another (Alexander, 1987). Ideological arguments are of a general nature as they extend beyond the framework of Fair Trade. These are answers of principle. This means that they are 'programmed' and are relatively immune to 'facts'. Although specific ideological presuppositions are more strongly associated with certain theoretical formulations than with others, each of these two analytical levels is relatively autonomous one from the other.

Generally speaking, economic debates focus on five main issues, which are obviously not totally independent from one another. The distinctions made below are exclusively for an analytical purpose:

- The distributive impact: does Fair Trade improve the living conditions of producers, especially the poorest? Does it contribute to marginalising other non-FT producers? etc.
- Allocative efficiency: does it distort market signals, such as price–quality relationship for instance? Does it lead to maintaining inefficient producers? etc.
- Transfer system efficiency: is it an efficient resource transfer system? Where does the surplus paid by consumers go? Is it a more efficient system than existing alternatives? etc.

- Control system efficiency: does it allow for an efficient follow up of the behaviours involved? For instance, does the system effectively identify and deal with abuses? etc.
- Global efficiency as economic policy: is it an alternative to existing economic policy instruments, or even to those that were suggested?

Here again, it must be said that it is anything but easy to test theoretical assumptions, as has been amply demonstrated by contemporary epistemology. Generally speaking, the emergence of 'facts' that contradict the theory is dealt with through *ad hoc assumptions* or '*immunizing stratagems*', to quote Popper; in other words, assumptions whose goal is to prevent rebuttal attempts. A prior study on the conditions of validity of the various theories or theoretical models is therefore required.

Finally, as far as empirical arguments are concerned, they are relatively autonomous from those of a theoretical or even ideological nature. Approaches with diametrically opposed underpinnings can, in some circumstances, arrive at the same empirical diagnosis. Conversely, the same facts can be the object of different theoretical interpretations. The remainder of this book aims to disentangle this web. This chapter presents the main arguments of principle against Fair Trade.

The Origins of a Debate: The Abolitionist Movement

Before addressing arguments of principle, a short historical detour is required in order to better set their background. The debate on a fairer international trade is not new. Yet there is no need to go back to the Scholasticism of medieval times for what constitutes a fair price. Fair Trade is very much an issue introduced by capitalism. Since its dark origin, described by Karl Marx (1887 [1867]) in his chapter on 'primitive accumulation', the issue of fairer international trade has been an ongoing one. Each time, the aim has been to denounce the asymmetric consequences of international trade as experienced by segments of the world labour force whose living conditions are considered particularly unbearable.

Already, at the end of the eighteenth century, British abolitionists had started asking for a boycott of sugar from the West Indies on the grounds that it was produced by slaves. This episode is narrated by African-Caribbean historian Eric Williams (1994 [1944]: 183) in his seminal *Capitalism and Slavery*, precisely in the chapter entitled 'The "Saints" and Slavery':

William Fox [an abolitionist] in 1792 informed the British people that in every pound of sugar they consumed two ounces of human flesh. By an elaborate mathematical computation it was estimated that if one family using five pounds of sugar a week would abstain for twenty-one months, one Negro would be spared enslavement and murder. The consumer of sugar was really 'the prime mover, the grand cause of all the horrible injustice'.

Since the British people could no longer do without sugar, the sugar brought in from the West Indies was to be substituted by sugar from India. This boycott was perceived, especially by the ladies of the abolitionist movement, as 'the safest, easiest and most effective manner' to fight slavery (Williams, 1994 [1944]: 184). In this pursuit, abolitionists spared no effort. They ran numerous sensitisation campaigns. They put up posters throughout Britain and produced pamphlets as well as other propaganda documents that had a more pedagogical slant. In short, they did everything possible to mobilise public opinion and win it over. According to Williams (1994 [1944]: 178), abolitionists led 'one of the greatest propaganda movements of all time'.

The interesting aspect of this movement is the ambivalence of its main actors.[1] Williams argues that the abolitionist lobby did not believe in the notion of equality between black people and white people. In fact, the idea of black emancipation was only accepted from 1823 with the caveat that it was to be introduced gradually. But the worst problem lay elsewhere. It is a fact that abolitionists were not very consistent in their approach. They encouraged the British public to boycott sugar from the West Indies. If they had been consistent, states Eric Williams, they would also have called for the boycott of products from Brazil and Cuba, which both employed slave labour. On the contrary, they approved of this trade, just as they kept quiet about the issue of the cotton imported from the United States which British industries could not do without. In the latter case, their argument was that the slaves who produced American cotton were not under the authority of the British Empire and that, as far as they were concerned, no major exaction had been documented. According to Williams, the abolitionists seemed to overlook the fact that the chairs they sat on were made of mahogany from Cuba, just as their desks were made of rosewood from Brazil. But they apparently were not keen 'to go round and inquire into the pedigree of every chair and table' (Williams,

1994 [1944]: 190). What the abolitionists did not understand or refused to accept is that British capitalism simply could not do without slavery.

As Eric Williams explains, history overplayed humanistic sentiment as well as the role of abolitionists in the abolition of both the slave trade and slavery itself. In reality, through slavery, the abolitionists wanted to challenge the monopoly granted to the British West Indies, colonies that had stopped being profitable according to British industrialists. This is evidenced by the fact that after the formal abolition of the slave trade, they continued to oppose plantation owners from the West Indies although these no longer used slaves. 'Where, before 1833, they had boycotted the British slave owner, after 1833 they espoused the cause of the Brazilian slave owner' (Williams, 1994 [1944]: 188). Many actors of the abolitionist movement had stakes in the East Indies and the monopoly granted to products coming from the West Indies did not play in their favour. They therefore decided to challenge this monopoly. The fight against slavery provided this generous humanistic excuse. Capitalism and the abolitionist movement walked hand in hand. Williams gives the example of James Cropper, an abolitionist and economist who owned stakes in India. To show his support to the anti-slavery movement, he allegedly offered his supporters and members of the British parliament small bottles of coffee and sugar produced with free labour. According to Williams, Cropper's propaganda was such that even his cutlery was engraved with depictions of chained black slaves.

Williams' arguments anticipate the criticism levied at Fair Trade today by some authors of the left, namely that under capitalism, hardly anything is produced or exchanged fairly. Karl Marx actually wrote that capital came to the world 'dripping from head to foot, from every pore, with blood and dirt' (1887 [1867]: ch. 31), so much so that the boycott or 'buycott' of specific products on humanitarian grounds is a 'pious and silly crusade', to use a contemporary phrase quoted by Williams (1994 [1944]: 183).

Nowadays, Fair Trade consists in selective purchase initiatives ('buycott') or in positive discrimination towards specific products. In the era of the abolitionists, 'buycott' was the counterpart of boycott. Beyond the similar methods and issues, what is certainly amazing is that, since then, the same unequal exchange relations continue between almost the same geographical zones. This shows that slavery was more a symptom than the cause of the problem. Hence the somewhat paradoxical nature of the Fair Trade movement, as it wants to reduce global poverty but accepts the structure of the international division of labour. Would Fair Trade therefore represent a new iteration of the abolitionist movement? In any case, the parallel is striking.[2]

The Origins of a Debate: The Tradition of Free Trade

Besides the abolitionist movement, the Fair Trade Debate (1870–90) provided yet another historical precedent to the Fair Trade issue. It seems that it is in the framework of this debate that the opposition between free trade and protectionism was structured.

On this point, the story begins with the tradition of free trade. Its influence has grown consistently since the Scottish economist and philosopher Adam Smith, considered as the founding father of modern economic science, published in 1776 his work entitled *An Inquiry into the Nature and Causes of the Wealth of Nations*. Just as the official history of capitalism conveys the false theory that free trade was the strategy followed in the past by countries that are rich today, the official history of political economy as written by the 'victors' also teaches us that Adam Smith is the founding father of the free trade tradition. Smith certainly set the standard of economic liberalism. For him to be seen as a wholehearted partisan of free trade however, not to mention the founding father of this tradition, a good deal of nit-picking and rhetorical contortions must have been undertaken by eminent historians of political economy.

In *The Tradition of Free Trade* (2004), Lars Magnusson dismantles this theory in a very convincing manner. To begin with, he points out that the arguments in favour of free trade existed before Smith. This was actually vigorously claimed by Joseph Schumpeter, an author who saw Smith as an economist lacking in originality, although he managed to faithfully reflect the spirit of his times.[3]

Magnusson's analysis is generally similar to that of Schumpeter while completing it on some points. According to Magnusson, there were not one but several faces of Adam Smith. Such was his influence that in most countries (England, the United States, Sweden, Germany), his intellectual authority was mobilised both by the supporters and adversaries of free trade. The controversy around the Smith persona finds part of its origin in his methodological approach.

According to Magnusson, Smith saw a significant difference between the general principles and practical problems of economic policy. For Smith, economic principles could not logically produce economic policy recommendations that would be valid in all circumstances. The specific histories, the role of institutions, human nature, unforeseen consequences (symbolised by the notorious 'invisible hand') are, according to Smith, so many parameters that can create a gap between the general principles and the practical uses that these can lead to; hence, from a methodological point of view, his frequent digressions and his use of historical illustrations.

Thus, Smith considered the 'perfect freedom of trade' as the 'general principle of wealth and opulence'. Nevertheless, in terms of economic policy, the adoption of free trade should generally be balanced against other considerations relating to national sovereignty or national interests. Smith was thus in favour of the British Navigation Protection Acts on grounds of defence and national security. Then, there are circumstances when, according to him, a breach of the principles of free trade was justified, and others when there was 'matter of deliberation'. More broadly speaking, Smith approved of state intervention (1) for activities where the individual has an imperfect knowledge and (2) in cases where the exercise of natural freedom can threaten society at large.

Initially, following the publication of the *Wealth of Nations*, Smith's works were not yet approached from the perspective of his leanings towards free trade. Quite to the contrary, Smith was perceived by his contemporaries as the inventor of a new system that was superior to mercantilism and whose originality was based on the principle of the division of labour in which labour is the only source of value. Mercantilism is generally described as a doctrine that considers trade as a zero sum game, the objective being to gather the maximum gold possible thanks to trade surpluses. From a normative point of view, this vision was problematic for two reasons at least: on the one hand, it represented an argument against free trade and, on the other, it implied protectionist leanings that often led to wars and threatened the international order. Smith rejected this doctrine by arguing that it confused wealth with the accumulation of monetary reserves. In fact, the substance of the mercantilist argument was more sophisticated than this caricature, as Keynes admitted later (see Hudson, 2009).

But more importantly, the Smithian approach does not provide a definite argument in favour of commercial openness. As Magnusson states, there is no distinction for Smith between domestic and foreign trade. The latter was perceived as a specific case where the principle of division of labour could apply. International trade was meant to benefit the trade stakeholders due to international specialisation. In turn this was to encourage productivity and economic growth. This dynamic vision of international trade was named the 'productive theory' of trade.

Smith, however, had a second vision of trade – the *vent for surplus theory* – which was rejected by economists such as John Stuart Mill due to its mercantilist 'remnants'. According to Smith, international trade enables a nation to export its surplus products and to capitalise on them by swapping them against products for which domestic demand exists. This vision seems to contradict the first. Hence the unease it long caused partisans of Adam Smith as founder of free trade. According to Magnusson, describing Smith as someone with mercantilist leanings is only problematic if he is considered as a supporter of laissez-faire and the inventor of the doctrine of comparative advantage. He argues that Smith's 'productive theory' was never developed with a view to producing the comparative advantage doctrine, as Smith had doubts about its relevance given the context of his time.

The principle of comparative advantage

The comparative advantage doctrine first appeared under the pen of Robert Torrens before being popularised by David Ricardo. It provides the main argument in favour of free trade and the international division of labour based on specialisation. To understand the comparative advantage logic, one has to approach it from the perspective of the notion of absolute advantage. In a context where international trade is based on absolute costs, a nation that produces goods at a lesser cost than other nations, for instance, has little interest in trading with them. Conversely, a nation that has no absolute advantage should, in all logic, have nothing to export. At a time when England was considered the 'workshop of the world', this concept was clearly not in line with the prevailing free trading mood.

To justify the benefits of free trade, Ricardo developed the idea of comparative advantage. He gave the example of cloth and wine to show that although England was less competitive than Portugal on each of these products taken in isolation, it was still in the country's interest to maintain trade relations with Portugal. The example chosen by Ricardo distorted reality (at the time, England was more competitive than Portugal from an industrial point of view – see Hudson, 2009). It is his counter-intuitive conclusion, however, that grabs the attention. Nowadays, in the field of family economics, comparative advantage is also used to justify the domestic division of labour: even if men can be more efficient at the market and in household chores, the economic rationale recommends that they specialise in market activities while women specialise in 'domestic production'. In this way, the 'welfare' of the household is 'maximised'! This may seem like a caricature, but it is the very essence of part of the dominant economic theory. In spite of the many subsequent theoretical developments within the neoclassical research programme, arguments in favour of trade liberalisation have a rather precarious foundation (see Box 3.1).

Box 3.1   Arguments in favour of free trade and
their limits in the context of developing countries

The main theoretical arguments in favour of free trade are generally based on efficiency considerations and not on its impact on economic growth:

- static and dynamic gains of specialisation according to comparative advantage;
- market openness, boosting foreign demand for domestic products, possibilities for economies of scale;
- availability of low-cost inputs, which reduces the production costs;
- introduction of competition between domestic companies, which increases efficiency.

Trade liberalisation can no doubt strengthen economic growth through different channels. However, when taking into account market 'imperfections', the possibility of trade liberalisation hampering economic growth can also be demonstrated. In other words, the relation between trade liberalisation and economic growth is all but unequivocal from a theoretical point of view.

Besides, the theoretical models that demonstrate the higher efficiency of free trade are based on assumptions that do not match the structural specificities of developing countries:

- the hypothesis of the full use of human resources (no unemployment or under-employment);
- the hypothesis of the lack of rigidity on the supply side: for instance, with trade openness, exporting firms can quickly increase their production and adjust to the evolution of global demand;
- the hypothesis of an efficient risk market: for instance, in circumstances when prices are volatile, there are insurance mechanisms available to producers;
- the hypothesis of compensation for the 'losers' of trade liberalisation;
- the hypothesis that said compensation can be implemented without involving costs.

Beyond the classical argument in favour of the protection of infant industries, we can add that free trade supporters do not pay sufficient attention to value chain phenomena. Assuming that free trade keeps its promises, it is possible that its benefits are monopolised by the oligopolies and oligopsonies that are active along value chains. Though this fails to note the important share that customs revenue can sometimes represent in the financing of public expenditure.

Source: Stiglitz and Charlton (2005: 24–33).

Consolidating the tradition of free trade

The least we can say is that Adam Smith was a pragmatic thinker who did not shy away from using common sense. This is no doubt what explains the ambivalent nature of his work and heritage. For some, Smith was a radical. For others, he was a libertarian who was suspicious about state intervention. Beyond his critique of mercantilism, the image of Smith as a eulogist of commercial laissez-faire owes a great deal to his position at the time in favour of the liberalisation of wheat imports, a measure which, according to him, benefited the poor. Gradually, at the turn of the nineteenth century, the image of Smith as a radical and 'friend of the poor' started being deconstructed to be replaced by that of a Smith who advocates total free trade. Smith as founder of political economy and economic liberalism was popularised by the Manchester 'School' and, ironically, by what was called 'evangelist political economy'. Outside of the United Kingdom, advocates of the *American System*, of which Alexander Hamilton was one of the eminent representatives, built on Smith in order to back arguments such as the protection of infant industries. Magnusson (2004: 123) sums up this argument as follows:

> As the American case makes clear, it is perhaps more appropriate to speak of a process of 'translation', in which the original meanings of concepts and theories were transformed and put to work in a new context. Hence, in the United States and elsewhere, there was certainly a lot of open and explicit criticism directed against Smith and Ricardo and the tradition of British political economy. However, it is more interesting to note how American economists used Smith and others to argue against total free trade and in favour of at least some governmental intervention. As we saw, until the 1840s at least, it was possible to argue that Smithian economics as well as classical political economy was open to different interpretations. It was not until later that the invention of a tradition of absolute free trade dating back to Smith won the day.

According to Magnusson, free trade is the cornerstone on which modern economic science was built. He argues that the free trade vs protectionism controversy is the most important debate that economists took part in before the Keynesian revolution. It is precisely in the context of what was called the Fair Trade Debate (1870–90) that free trade was consolidated as a doctrine, Smith having been used as the 'straw man':

> the controversy over the fair trade movement with the help of popularisers as well as professional economists played its own role in establishing the view that there existed a distinctive tradition of free trade discourse leading back to Adam Smith. (Magnusson, 2004: 68)

It is important to note that free trade opponents built on the notion of 'Fair Trade' to defend protectionist and imperialistic positions. As Magnusson (2004: 65) points out: 'in the 1890s the fair trade movement became a part of a movement for imperial reform and colonial expansion which achieved its real triumph only after the turn of the new century'. This no doubt is the reason that Fair Trade does not have the same connotation among Anglo-Saxons as *Commerce* équitable does for the Francophone. Whatever the case may be, with the tradition of free trade, we hold the second piece of doctrinal criticism of Fair Trade.

Free Trade vs Fair Trade: The Neoliberal Critique

The harshest criticism of Fair Trade to date has no doubt been levied by the Adam Smith Institute. This British think tank, which hails from a classical liberalism tradition, published a document during Fair Trade Fortnight in the United Kingdom written by Marc Sidwell and with a self-explanatory title: *Unfair Trade* (Sidwell, 2008). If the timing of its publication helped it achieve tremendous media coverage, we must acknowledge that it is far from representing archetypal academic research. It would be more accurate to describe it as a pamphlet. Indeed, its arguments are mostly built around biased quotes (Smith, 2008) and positions of principle, rather than on a rational assessment. Nevertheless, some of its ideas are worthy of note, as it perfectly typifies the logic of neoliberal criticism.

According to the neoliberal doctrine, the liberalisation of the markets (or of international trade more precisely) is the best way to reach the two objectives of economic efficiency and social justice. This assumption is what opposes it to the Fair Trade movement. Another source of divergence is that the neoliberal evaluation model places a greater focus on 'processes' (liberalisation) whereas that of the Fair Trade advocates gives more importance to distributive 'consequences' (distribution of gains, poverty, etc.). Neoliberal critics accuse Fair Trade of restricting consumer choices, promoting an unacceptable political agenda and *in fine* failing to provide a better alternative than free trade.

Fair Trade fails to consider consumer sovereignty

The debate on Fair Trade goes beyond the opposition between specific political conceptions of how to live together. It refers to profound divergences on philosophical, moral and religious dimensions. This at least seems to be the case in the United Kingdom where a new Fair Trade debate is actually taking place.[4] A programme director of the Institute of Economic Affairs, a British think tank with neoliberal leanings, explains that church-goers in the diocese in which he lived had told him (1) that not purchasing Fair Trade products is a sin worse than theft, because doing otherwise amounts to bleeding the poor and (2) that products with the Fairtrade label are the only fair ones for the poor (Booth, 2008). Here is another example: a philosopher argues that consumers are morally obligated to buy Fair Trade products and that governments are morally obligated to support the movement (Philips, 2009). In their communications, labelling initiatives also present similar arguments. Statements such as these can be read: 'In conclusion, the only acceptable price for coffee is more than ever that charged by Fair Trade.'[5] The unease caused by this new black and white approach can be sensed in many writings. It is, however, in the neoliberal critique that this aspect is most obvious. Indeed, this critique is ill at ease with the following three statements: (1) Fair Trade is the only approach that leads to the payment of a 'fair' price, (2) its impact is more significant than that of existing alternatives and (3) those who do not buy Fair Trade products inevitably pay unfair prices.

It is therefore not surprising that Fair Trade is perceived by neoliberal critics as a breach of individual freedoms due to its very approach. Its dominant position in the sector of 'ethical' consumption is strongly challenged. According to Marc Sidwell, its protagonists exert moral pressure on consumers who then feel compelled to buy FT products. The reasoning is that consumers should 'maximise' the funds they allocate to 'ethical' actions (for instance world hunger, the environment, child labour, etc.). To this end, one should not impose a given 'ethical' initiative to consumers, but leave them with a broad range of choices that can help them determine which initiative is the best (namely that which would enable the most efficient transfer to the cause they wish to support). To simplify, *Homo Economicus* has a demand for 'ethical' products, but would like to have the broadest choice possible. Beyond that, we must point out that neoliberal critics are not particularly convinced of the efficiency of Fair Trade as a resource transfer system. Its assumption is that the same results can be achieved at a lesser cost. Indeed, a recurring argument is that charity would be a more efficient transfer system than Fair Trade.

This said, Marc Sidwell nevertheless acknowledges that Fair Trade is an example of voluntary exchange as codified by the neoliberal doctrine. Therefore, consumers retain sovereignty and have the right to do whatever they please with their money. But his concern lies with the fact that Fair Trade protagonists allegedly try to 'circumvent' the market by engaging in 'social blackmail'. They not only receive government subsidies, but also force the latter to guarantee a market niche for them.

On this point, we must recognise that FT products are increasingly in a monopolistic position in non-market institutions – ministries, parliaments, school canteens, etc. Along these lines, the European Parliament actually asked the European Commission to encourage Fair Trade in public procurement procedures.[6] In such cases, there is, according to Marc Sidwell (2008: 23), 'a disconnect between buying Fair Trade, presented as a consumer choice that will correct a market failure, and lobbying government in the belief that free markets must be stopped by law'.

The following is a symbol of this contradiction: in November 2007, Douwe Egberts lodged a suit against the province of Groningen (Netherlands) after it put out a tender for the supply of coffee meeting Fair Trade standards. The Sara Lee subsidiary argued that the province had discriminated against it by giving preference to products that meet Fairtrade criteria. As a result, candidates whose coffee is certified by competing organisations (in this case Douwe Egberts working with UTZ Certified) will be excluded. The request was nevertheless rejected.[7] Understandably, this decision was welcomed with a great deal of relief and seen as a major victory by Fair Trade protagonists and their proponents who immediately published a letter asking that Douwe Egberts and others take notice of the 'choice' of public authorities in favour of Fair Trade. The greatest irony is that this decision of the court felt like a bitter pill to Nico Roozen, cofounder of the Fairtrade label and board chair at UTZ Certified. According to him, the UTZ Certified label provides stronger guarantees in terms of sustainable development than the Fairtrade label![8]

Neoliberal critics scored a major point when they pointed to the willingness of the Fair Trade movement to bend the arm of governments, so that what was initially to be a matter of consumer choice ends up as a legislative *fait accompli*. But they lost a great deal of credibility when, after having denounced this contradiction, when they shamelessly and deliberately publicised alternative companies or approaches in what were presented as 'academic' documents (see for example Berndt, 2007; Sidwell, 2008).[9]

Fair Trade is protectionism

According to advocates of the neoliberal doctrine, the political agenda of Fair Trade is not acceptable. In actual fact, it is akin to a new Trojan horse in favour of protectionism. This point of view is especially defended by Jagdish Bhagwati. According to him, the phrase 'Fair Trade' (which is generally translated into French as 'Commerce équitable') is an ambiguous concept due to the several definitions it is given.[10] He lists three main ones.

According to him, the first meaning dates back to the nineteenth century. More precisely, it appeared in the United Kingdom in the context of the 'Fair Trade Debate' as we have seen, a period when protectionism was spreading among the United Kingdom's trade partners, like 'a weed from the soil', to quote an expression used by free trade proponents (Magnusson, 2004). The concept of 'Fair Trade' expressed the notion of a request for trade reciprocity. A country practices *unfair* trade as soon as its trade barriers are considered excessive by the United Kingdom in light of its own free trade policy. In the 1980s, Japan stood accused by the United States. Nowadays, it is China's turn to be accused of having an 'unfair' trade strategy by the world's First Power. In fact, as a reprisal against a Yuan perceived to be undervalued, the House of Representatives passed the Currency Reform for Fair Trade Act in September 2010, though this was finally overturned by the Senate.

The second definition has a more recent origin and conveys the idea that trade between nations that have different standards in terms of environmental protection and worker rights is 'unfair'. From this perspective, free trade is unfavourable to rich countries, as poor countries practising social and environmental 'dumping' have competitive advantages that rich countries can never match, except through levelling down.

Another definition, which is closer to that of Fair Trade protagonists, expresses a demand for a fair price for producers and wage workers. According to Bhagwati, this is an issue that was publicised by Oxfam and that we can trace back to Joseph Rowntree in the nineteenth century, when he advocated for a decent price for cocoa producers.

Bhagwati argues that the first two definitions clearly refer to protectionist strategies in disguise. As for the third, according to him, it only leads to protectionism when the aim is to replace conventional products by Fair Trade products. But, as Marc Sidwell argues, there is a risk that the Fair Trade movement will begin to gather a growing number of supporters who will challenge the current economic order and advocate a return to the long-gone era of market economy regulation. Indeed, the main argument of neoliberalism on Fair Trade is to say that it is economically inefficient and that free trade is a clearly superior alternative.

Free trade is the 'real' Fair Trade

The best empirical arguments in the world can probably never convince neoliberal critics of the legitimacy of Fair Trade. Nevertheless, it is entitled to insist on the need for Fair Trade protagonists to show more transparency and thoroughness when it comes to assessing its distributive impact. According to one passionate critic, when millions of lives are at stake, Fair Trade protagonists have a duty to be accountable by providing reliable information on gains received by producers of the South and on the destination of the transfer made by consumers (Griffith, 2009). This is at once a critique of principle and one of methodology. Many authors from the neoliberal trend criticised Fair Trade protagonists for their 'illiteracy' when it comes to discussing 'economics' (by which they mean neoclassical economics; see for example Brink, 2003), because they resort to anecdotes rather than more thorough methods, publish documents that were not vetted by impartial peer evaluation in line with academic standards and resort to *ad hominem* arguments to respond to criticism levelled at them (Brink, 2003; Griffith, 2009; Sidwell, 2008).

Beyond this, whatever the facts around Fair Trade, neoliberal critics have no intention of departing from free trade dogma. They delivered a verdict even before trying Fair Trade. This movement could only be a doomed attempt, as free trade is the remedy to the problems of workers and producers of the South. Nations that embraced free trade always knew how to come out on top. Those that remained poor, like most

African countries, are those that resisted the sirens of the free market for a long time. Therefore, Fair Trade is a superfluous luxury that we can do without provided that the conditions for genuine trade liberalisation are put into place in the South just as in the North. The solution is to make international trade 'freer', not 'fairer', as this term is defined by organisations such as FLO: *freer trade not fairer trade*, as the advocates of free trade say.

> The evidence is clear: free trade works. Developing countries that significantly lowered their trade barriers in the 1990s grew three times more quickly than those who did not. If we want to understand what keeps poor countries poor, the answer is not unfair trade terms imposed by big businesses and richer nations, nor is it solely developed world tariffs, but the resistance to free trade by their own leaders. (Sidwell, 2008: 20)

Beyond their blatant neglect of the deeply unbalanced and asymmetric nature of North–South trade relations, what is interesting in these arguments is the statement according to which recent history demonstrated a positive correlation between trade liberalisation and economic growth. In actual fact, it is the opposite of what an author like Dani Rodrik, an economist at Harvard University, has been endeavouring to demonstrate in a convincing manner for more than a decade. According to him, existing works in this field did not succeed in demonstrating that trade liberalisation promotes economic growth due to several conceptual weaknesses and to their lack of robustness (results vary depending on samples, periods, methods and indicators chosen) (Rodriguez and Rodrik, 2000). On the other hand, he argues, it is undeniable that the developing countries that most benefited from the gains of globalisation are those that introduced heterodox and gradualist economic policies in their approaches towards economic openness. Still, according to him, empirical data also showed that the vast majority of developing countries which, in recent history, followed the neoliberal orthodoxy, the notorious 'Washington Consensus', have had disastrous economic performances (see Box 3.2).

In other words, neoliberal criticism of Fair Trade is rather weak from a logical point of view. On the one hand, it cannot attack consumer choices without contradicting its support of the sacred principle of individual freedom. On the other, it cannot argue that it represents a better economic alternative *a priori* than the model promoted by Fair Trade, because its economic and social results so far are certainly not persuasive. Besides, at the risk of surprising both neoliberal criticism and its punch-bag, the fact is that Fair Trade is an extension of the logic of free trade and not an alternative to it. This point will be underscored in the next chapter. Nevertheless, there is a point on which neoliberal critics certainly deserve some attention: the assessment of the distributive impact of Fair Trade.

Box 3.2   Paradoxes of neoliberal orthodoxy

In the framework of the neoclassical research programme, the relation between trade liberalisation and economic growth is hardly unequivocal, but rather theoretically ambiguous. This is an issue that can therefore only be 'resolved' by resorting to the tribunal of 'facts'. As the following paradoxes reveal, one of the main lessons taught by recent history is that liberalism in the realm of economic policy is neither necessary, nor sufficient for successful integration into globalisation.

Developing countries that are perceived as having had a successful integration into globalisation – China, India and Vietnam for example – are, paradoxically, those that had the most rigid barriers at the start of the 1990s. China and Vietnam were not even WTO members at the time. They joined the organisation in 2001 and 2007 respectively. The second paradox, for a country such as China, is that trade liberalisation started about 15 years after the beginning of rapid and sustained growth. The third paradox is that countries that made the most significant efforts at trade liberalisation in line with the neoliberal orthodoxy, namely those of Latin America, recorded poor economic performances, not to mention a worsening of inequalities. The fourth paradox is that most developing countries in Africa, Asia and Latin America recorded their best performances between 1950 and 1973. Ironically, this was a period when developing countries adopted industrialisation strategies based on import substitution. This was completely at odds with neoliberal orthodoxy, hence their being called into question in the 1980s. The fifth paradox is that the period 1950–73, which represents the 'Golden age' of Keynesianism, was the most prosperous period in world economic history, with a world economic growth (GDP/capita) of around 3 per cent per year. Such a level had never been reached before. It has not been achieved again since then. The sixth paradox is that since the neoliberal turn, there have never been such a large number of financial and banking crises.

Source: Rodrik (2007a, 2007b).

The Alterglobalist Critique: the Flaws of the Promotion of Social Justice Via the Free Market

If most alterglobalist movements and other sympathisers aspire to fairer global trade, they are not necessarily all satisfied with the response provided by the Fair Trade movement in its Fairtrade version. Alterglobalist critics challenge the relevance of the vision of capitalism at the root of the FT model. They also denounce the inconsistency between the principles and ambitions of the movement on the one hand, and the means it uses on the other.

Fair Trade as a euphemism for the structures and imperatives of capitalism

One of the premises of Fair Trade is that trade relations between North and South must be changed in order for the gains deriving from it to benefit the latter more. Its protagonists thus feel that by promoting the adoption of new modes of consumption, it will be possible to reach this end. This approach was criticised by some authors due to its 'neo-Smithian' vision of the capitalist system (Fridell, 2007). In the language of authors in the Marxist lineage, this label symbolises the vision initially developed by Adam Smith, according to which capitalism would have 'originated' and been structured by a division of labour based on market exchange (Brenner, 1977). In the *Wealth of Nations*, Adam Smith demonstrates that the division of labour is a source of wealth creation – it increases labour productivity – and therefore of economic growth. He also underscores that the division of labour is limited by the size of the market. Thus, the development of trade is meant to increase labour productivity through an efficient division of labour. This is the Smithian 'productive theory' that I alluded to earlier.

According to Robert Brenner, Smithian reasoning takes three crucial conditions for granted. First, it assumes that the labour force can move freely in response to market signals. This is only possible when the labour force is free (no slavery, no servitude, and no forced labour). It also implies that the division of labour enables a labour productivity increase. This is the case only when free workers are gathered within *production units* with means of production made available for that purpose. Indeed, the existence of several small owners of means of production does not encourage specialisation or the adoption of new methods of production. Finally, it implies that there is continuous pressure towards an increase in labour productivity. This was not the case until the advent of capitalism.

In fact, according to Brenner, in the line of Karl Marx and Karl Polanyi, the economic development model described by Adam Smith presupposes social relations of production that are specific to the capitalist system: private property and the 'commodification' of labour. Capitalism presupposes on the one hand a free labour force and on the other a separation between workers and the means of production. In the capitalist system, as Henri Nadel points out, 'man with labour power must necessarily have no other commodity to sell but this strength, and no other means to survive without alienating it' (1994: 129). Likewise, owners of means of production must compete with one another in order to preserve their means of production. These are the structural contradictions that would generate economic growth as well as its related exploitation and inequalities.

Thus, according to Brenner, and contrary to the claims of Adam Smith and some neo-Marxist approaches (dependency and world-system theorists), the development of trade alone cannot be the historical 'origin' of capitalism: it 'does not determine a transition to new class relations in which the continuing development of the productive forces via accumulation and innovation become both possible and necessary' (Brenner, 1977: 40). Therefore, according to Brenner, the *origins* of capitalism as well as its *economic development model* must be analysed above all from the angle of social relations of production – namely class conflicts.[11]

From this angle, unequal exchange cannot be considered as the *fundamental* reason for the development/underdevelopment of specific regions of the globe. This is a phenomenon that always existed. But the specificity of capitalism lies in the fact that the levied rent contributes to further capital accumulation instead of war financing, kingdom consolidation or ostentatious consumption, as was the case with the economic systems that preceded it. It is this indefinite accumulation of capital that is the cornerstone of modern economic growth. Thus, according to this perspective, it would seem unrealistic to want to modify trade relations while maintaining intact the nature of the social relations of production.

For authors such as Fridell (2007), this is one of the major contradictions of Fair Trade: its protagonists attempt to fight against the free market while staying within it – to paraphrase Michael Barratt Brown (1993) – and while accepting the structure of capitalistic social relations of production. They would describe the phenomenon of exploitation as a distortion brought into the market resulting from the 'attitude' of 'unscrupulous' groups. According to him, this vision plays down the importance of the 'structural imperatives' of capitalism: competition, accumulation of capital, innovation and profit maximisation. It would also tend to consider social relations of production – and their related struggles – not as the *starting point* of capitalist development, but as one of its *consequences*. As Fridell wrote (2007: 14–15), the Fair Trade movement :

> is premised on the belief that global inequality and injustice can be combated with radical reforms to trade, at the level of both individual firms and the international trade regime, without a fundamental transformation of political power, class relations, and property ownership within the states that constitute the world system.

But he argues that this position is not tenable, as it is based on a superficial analysis: multinationals and major capitalist actors are less to blame; rather, it is the system based on private property and the commodification of labour that is problematic. Moreover, he argues, these limitations manifest themselves in the increasingly large gap between the principles of Fair Trade and the reality of their implementation.

On the 'unholy alliance' with large distributors and multinationals

To achieve the recognised media and marketing success that it enjoys today, Fair Trade has had to strike an alliance with large distributors (namely supermarkets and hypermarkets) as well as agrifood multinationals. This strategy is deliberate and asserted by labelling initiatives. Indeed, they chose to standardise FT products as much as possible. This implies that these should be commercialised in structures where average consumers usually shop. According to their logic, selling remotely or via specialised shops does not promote the visibility of FT products and, therefore, their commercialisation. Standardisation also means that FT products must be made available by major agrifood brands. For example, FT coffee should be served to consumers by giants such as Starbucks or McDonald's.

Labelling initiatives put forward two main arguments to defend this alliance with large distribution and agrifood multinationals. First, Fair Trade runs the risk of remaining in a tiny 'niche' if its products are only sold through alternative channels. A consequence of this is that its impact would be limited from the point of view of developing the South. In contrast, the standardisation of FT products enables a transition to a higher level. It boosts sales and thus, increases the budgetary envelope reaching producers and workers of the South. Second, standardising FT products helps to further sensitise consumers on the living conditions of workers and producers in the South.

However, these arguments on efficiency are not accepted by alterglobalist critics, who resort to a logic of principle. According to this perspective, the alliance of labelling initiatives with large distributors and agrifood multinationals is an inherent contradiction: businesses that have a questionable ethical record have no business dealing with Fair Trade. Between Nestlé, caught red-handed trying to sell out-of-date baby milk to Colombians, McDonald's, considered by some alterglobalist activists as the symbol of 'junk food' and precarious working conditions, and Starbucks, the coffee giant that stands accused of *dumping* practices to shut out its rivals and trying to take intellectual property rights from Ethiopian producers on their coffee, the list of new members in the FT system with an unflattering ethical record has become longer in recent times (Jacquiau, 2006; Karpyta, 2009). As far as large distributors are concerned, the global giant Wal-Mart has also started providing FT products (see Box 3.3).

How can labelling initiatives trade with actors whose economic, social and environmental practices are criticised worldwide? How can it be that they work hand in hand with actors often considered as responsible for the low remuneration received by producers and workers in the South and the North? Naomi Klein's *No Logo* (2009) is without a doubt the best-known book among those that exposed these contradictions. In France, Christian Jacquiau's investigation (2006) fits perfectly into this framework. Hence the hostile reception from the Fairtrade sphere.

Fair Trade: a concept of variable geometry

Looking at it closely, it is essentially the notion of Fair Trade as defined and implemented by FLO which is considered problematic by alterglobalist critics. On this point, we can list three major objections that no doubt relate to different ideological and moral conceptions on one side and the other (see Miller, 2010; Pedregal, 2007).

First, for some authors and for most alternative trade organisations, 'product' certification is not consistent from a logical and moral perspective compared with the certification of 'organisations'. By certifying products, labelling initiatives may enable companies with unethical practices to sell FT products. This contributes to making them look good in the eyes of the public at a truly insignificant cost, since they are not required to

---

Box 3.3   Wal-Mart: a controversial giant in the small world of Fair Trade

Wal-Mart Stores, Inc. was founded in 1969, seven years after the first Wal-Mart store opened. This global leader of large distribution owns 8,300 facilities (supermarkets, discount stores, Sam's Club warehouses, etc.) spread all over the world – with 4,300 based in the United States. In April 2008, it started distributing its own FT-certified coffee. FT bananas and FT wine can also be found on the shelves of some of its establishments.

In terms of both sales and employment, Wal-Mart is considered the largest company in the world. In 2009, *Fortune* estimated its sales at $408 billion. This is roughly equivalent to the GDP of the 49 LDCs in 2007. It is also the largest private employer in the United States, with 1.4 million workers, and the largest private employer in Mexico. From the point of view of ethics, Wal-Mart is mostly renowned for its anti-trade union stand and restrictive trade practices. In the United States, it provoked a campaign from many detractors under the banner of 'Wake up Wal-Mart'. It is criticised for (1) paying its employees wages that are barely higher than the poverty line, especially the full-time staff, (2) not providing them with social security, (3) passing on the cost of social security to taxpayers, (4) discriminating against women and (5) forcing suppliers to sell at the lowest possible prices, even if it forces these to relocate to countries such as China or resort to illegal immigrant labour or child labour. In spite of that, it would seem that thanks to its economic 'management' model, Wal-Mart saved the average American household close to $2,500 in 2006. However, these figures are provided by a study commissioned by the multinational itself. Whatever the case may be, Wal-Mart proudly displays its sustainability programme on its website as well as the many awards received in this framework. Wal-Mart was sued for discrimination by a group of employees led by a certain Betty Dukes. Their number is estimated at 1.5 million! But their case was dismissed by the United States Supreme Court. More recently, Wal-Mart was accused of selling misleadingly labelled 'organic' pork in China![12]

Source: Wal-Mart (Wal-Mart Corporate Facts), *Fortune 500* and 'Wake up Wal-Mart' websites.

---

commit on large amounts (some authors speak of *Greenwashing*).[13] Better yet, entry into the FT system is compatible with breaches of FT principles and standards in the framework of activities and products not covered by FT certification. Thus, to take the case of McDonald's, the company is considered Fair Trade provided that it sells FT-certified coffee, but regardless of the quality of its food or way it treats its employees or suppliers. On the other hand, it is no longer considered Fair Trade when it sells non-FT-certified coffee, burgers or fries. More generally, product certification gives specific economic actors with a controversial ethical history the chance to engage in Fair Trade for an insignificant part of their purchases while continuing with their objectionable practices of yesteryear for the rest. In contrast, according to alterglobalist critics, certification of 'organisations' in the WFTO fashion makes more sense as it guarantees that actors of the movement maintain consistent practices that comply with the requirements of principle in this solidarity approach at all levels of value chains and in their various activities.

Second, the fact that the fairness requirement is addressed only from a North–South perspective is considered problematic. Why not an 'all fair' approach – North–North, South–South, North–South? The answer from labelling initiatives is that their priority is developing countries, as developed countries have enough resources to deal with the problems faced by their workers in the framework of globalisation. Alterglobalist critics argue that this is not consistent however. In the North, farmers fall victim to the practices of large distributors who increase their margins at their expense. Workers are also at the mercy of multinationals when these decide to systematically reduce their costs. Labelling initiatives should also speak up against such practices if they are to remain faithful to their principles. The question, therefore, is the following: does the concern to help producers and workers of the South justify labelling initiatives in turning a blind eye on the exploitation of producers and workers of the North by their 'allies' of large distribution and the agrifood industry? The problem also exists in the framework of South–South trade, even though very few authors mention it.

Third, the broadening of Fair Trade to encompass plantations is generally interpreted by alterglobalist critics as a negation of its original principles. Indeed, alternative trade approaches historically targeted small producer organisations. For their part, FLO and labelling initiatives justify the inclusion of plantations in terms of the concern to address the situation of landless workers who are generally made poor through exploitation by plantation owners. In their case, FT standards include, among others, the payment of decent wages, the prohibition of forced labour and child labour, trade union freedom, and the adoption of health and safety measures in favour of workers. This is why a large share of FT products (cut flowers, sugar, bananas and tea in particular) are imported from plantations based in various developing countries.

What needs to be understood here is that plantations are often perceived as a remnant of colonial practices that led to the dispossession of indigenous people in terms of both land and rights. As an example, Chiquita, the world leader of the banana trade held or controlled close to 85 per cent of available land in 1954 for growing this fruit in the main producing countries of Latin America, with the exception of Ecuador. In fact, when the government of Guatemala wanted to push its land reform by attacking Chiquita's interests, the CIA (Central Intelligence Agency) led a secret operation to topple it (Myers, 2004: 43ff.).

There is also the fact that the inclusion of plantations leads to a bias in the Fair Trade approach, as multinationals prefer to work with them rather than with a multitude of small organisations of producers who often live far from the main roads. For these multinationals, collaboration with plantations presents multiple benefits: time gains, economies of scale, better guarantees in terms of quality and steady deliveries, etc. Another aspect of the debate relates to the issue of whether FLO has the capacity to enforce these standards in such a context and to respond on a daily basis to repeated violations of workers' rights.

The risk of dilution of the Fairtrade label

According to alterglobalist critics, a major risk is posed by the difficulty of telling the difference between companies that are morally committed to the movement for fairer international trade and those that are only engaged in Fair Trade for opportunistic reasons: the 'dilution' of the Fairtrade label. According to them, there is a danger that the 'Fair' put in the hands of labelling initiatives might end up being a *'business'* more than anything else. Large distribution actors and multinationals using practices that have been globally denounced adhere to the system to get twice the benefits: maintaining, or increasing their usual margins on this new market and improving their image in the eyes of the public. This would tend to *compromise* the image of Fair Trade. The dilution of the Fairtrade label is also increased by the development of new competing labels. The effect of this is to *confuse* the Fair Trade message, as indicated among others by an opinion poll conducted in France. It would seem that only 13 per cent of the French people know the difference between the many labels that claim to practise Fair Trade.[14]

The Point of View of Degrowth

Among alterglobalist critics, a form of critique with environmentalist undertones deserves particular attention due to the originality of its assumption: the *degrowth* movement. This perspective is notable in France. Its partisans are self-proclaimed 'growth objectors' who radically challenge the contemporary productivist model and its corollary, the relentless quest for economic growth.

Décroissance, Entropie-Écologie-Économie [*Degrowth: Entropy–Ecology–Economy*] (1995 [1979]), by the eminent Romanian economist Nicholas Georgescu-Roegen, is the theoretical basis of the degrowth movement. In this book, Georgescu-Roegen engages in an epistemological critique of neoclassical economics (and of Marxist economics to a lesser extent). According to him, neoclassical economics borrowed the mechanistic physics model but overlooked the revolutionary teachings of thermodynamics, which he describes as the 'physics of economic value'. He demonstrates that, unlike in mechanistic models, the economic process is subject to the law of entropy: this is an irreversible process consisting in transforming natural resources of *value* into *waste*. The perpetual quest for economic growth is bound to come to a halt sooner or later due – from the point of view of *inputs* – to the limited resources of the planet which are not all reproducible, and – from the point of view of *outputs* – to the irreversible destruction caused by the progress of civilisation (pollution, waste, etc.). From this perspective, degrowth is an inevitable process. Scientific and technical progress will not change this, according to Georgescu-Roegen. The more we consume, the more entropy increases. More generally, all our actions, including those we take to resist this entropy (recycling waste for instance), only serve to take it to a higher level. Zero growth, or the stationary state, cannot be envisaged either.

On this basis, growth objectors challenge the concept of 'development' and its underlying paradigm, 'developmentism', on the basis in particular of the deconstruction work undertaken by Serge Latouche in his numerous publications. Serge Latouche (2004) argues that under the appearance of universalism, development is in fact a Western belief saturated with ethnocentrism. Synonymous with the accumulation of capital, it is ultimately based on ever higher economic growth and its alleged benefits (the *trickle down effect*). From a practical standpoint, it leads to the creation of new artificial needs, to a worsening of social and economic inequalities and to the destruction of the environment. According to Serge Latouche, as developmentism fell into disrepute due to its obvious contradictions, its partisans sought to rehabilitate it by covering it in 'new clothing', thus ushering in the era of 'development with adjectives': that is, 'human', 'social', 'sustainable', 'self-centred', 'local', 'alternative' development, etc.

According to Serge Latouche, these phrases are ambiguous and semantically suspicious. He argues that 'human' development and 'social' development are redundant phrases, as development cannot but be social or human. As for 'sustainable' development, which is defined as a form of development that does not compromise the chances of future generations, he argues that it represents an oxymoron – the juxtaposition of two contradictory words – from the point of view of experience, as development in its reality is the very denial of ideals of social justice, the preservation of the environment and *in fine* of *joie de vivre*. Thus, according to Serge Latouche (2004: 87):

> it is high time we put an end to the stale language of developmentism. There is no other development than development. It is useless seeking a better one as, in theory, this one is already good. Another development would be meaningless.

What we need therefore is an 'alternative to development', such as 'friendly degrowth' and 'localism'.

By entering into the paradigm of sustainable development, Fair Trade still did not escape the wrath of degrowth partisans. Although they espouse many alterglobalist arguments, such as the opportunistic takeover of Fair Trade by the 'Big Capital', they go further yet (see Pedregal, 2006 for a presentation of these arguments). First, they challenge its 'consumerist' model. According to the degrowth movement, Fair Trade promotes more consumption to solve human problems. However, degrowth is not only inevitable, but also, in terms of a societal choice, the only means of maximising the life expectancy of humanity and of future generations. Besides, the ecological costs linked to international transport do not seem to be factored in by Fair Trade. By encouraging countries of the South to export specific goods (those produced in the North mainly), Fair Trade seems to paradoxically contribute to increasing human pressure on the environment. Finally, Fair Trade seems not to encourage relocation of production processes. It encourages producers in the South to promote cash crops at the expense of subsistence crops. This threatens their food sovereignty and slows the adoption of more autonomous modes of living. This strategy also contributes to the depletion of soils under the pressure of productivist agriculture.

Conclusion

The objections to Fair Trade that I have reviewed are often irreconcilable with one another because they stem from radically opposed doctrinal approaches. Nevertheless, whether or not we agree with their premises, each has an undeniable merit. Neoliberal critics had the merit of insisting on the preservation of consumer interests and on the need to assess the distributive impact of Fair Trade. This also applies to alterglobalist critics, who described the inconsistencies of Fair Trade which seeks to transform the free market while subscribing to its logic. Finally, there is the perspective of degrowth, which, while it is a minority view, forces us to think off the beaten track and to envisage other forms of *living together* that we are perhaps not yet ready to embrace.

In spite of their divergences, all these critics share a common feature: they assess Fair Trade based on the societal model that they each find desirable from their point of view as citizens of the North. To some extent, we have the impression that each of these approaches considers Fair Trade as a laboratory experiment that may enable us to decide between the various conceptions of societal choices involved. Most protagonists in this debate no doubt wish for a decrease of world poverty as well as better economic and social prospects for the South. In spite of this wave of sympathy, the *sui generis* perspective of countries of the South receives far less attention.

In other words, the problem with this critical literature is that it approaches the issue of Fair Trade essentially from the point of view of rich countries (consumer perception of the movement, tensions and controversies caused by the doctrinal evolution of Fair Trade, competition between labels, etc.). This bias is obviously understandable, as the future of Fair Trade depends on consumers and political actors based in the North taking ownership of it. However, this leads to overlooking the heterogeneity of developing countries and to a lack of focus on the gradual or distributive nature of this new development technology. Is Fair Trade a model applicable to all developing countries? Is it a long-term strategy that can be recommended for them? Does this movement not hide new forms of exploitation of the South by the North? Who benefits from it in the South? The remainder of this book focuses on a critical examination of these questions, which have thus far not received the analytical treatment they deserve.

4

Redeeming the Free Market as a Solution to Poverty: The Limitations of the FT Economic Model

The free market dictates that countries stick to what they are already good at. Stated bluntly, this means that poor countries are supposed to continue with their current engagement in low-productivity activities. But their engagement in those activities is exactly what makes them poor. If they want to leave poverty behind, they *have to* defy the market and do the more difficult things that bring them higher incomes – there are no two ways about it [...]

If [Samsung and Nokia] had faithfully followed market signals in the way developing countries are told by the Bad Samaritans, Nokia would still be felling trees and Samsung refining imported sugar cane. (Chang, 2008: 210, original italics)

According to Chang, nations whose economies developed have in common that most of them 'defied' the market. In other words, they rejected the imperatives and signals from the market, careless economic openness and the argument that they should irrevocably specialise in line with the principle of comparative advantage. He provides several examples, including that of Nokia. This Finnish company is currently one of the world leaders in the sector of mobile telephony. Yet Nokia's electronic subsidiary did not produce the slightest profit for 17 years, its activities being funded by other subsidiaries. According to Chang, if Finland had liberalised foreign direct investment and/or if Nokia had stopped subsidising this subsidiary, considered as non-profitable at the time, we would never have had the Nokia as 'icon' of globalisation as we know it.[1]

To discuss the limits of the FT model, we are going to elaborate on this notion of market 'defiance'. My chief argument will be to say that Fair Trade is an unsuitable response to poverty in the South, as it very much relies on free market logic. This approach certainly fits into the comparative advantage logic and could be discussed from that point of view. However, I am rather going to focus my arguments on its price theory, because it is on this level that protagonists of the movement made their main contributions. I will conclude this discussion with a critical evaluation of the literature dealing with the local impact of Fair Trade.

Limitations of Accounting for the 'Sustainable'

Fair Trade seeks to promote economic, social and environmental development in the South by offering better prices to small producers. To understand the logic of this approach, one must focus on the problems it is attempting to solve. The first is the high price *volatility* for products exported by small producers in the South. The recommended solution is to set a *guaranteed minimum price*. The second problem identified relates to the *low returns* of these exports. The solution offered consists in better assessing the costs involved in '*sustainable production*' and to include them in the calculation of the guaranteed minimum price. The implicit justification is that traders tend to save unduly on the cost of 'sustainable' environment and working conditions. The third problem is the *exploitation* of small producers by local intermediaries who are often described as 'coyotes'. Indeed, producers often fall into debt cycles that maintain them in a state of dependency towards intermediaries. The solution given is to remove the intermediaries from the value chains or, at least, to encourage them *nolens volens* to use fairer trade practices. The strategy of 'euthanasia of intermediaries'[2] is orchestrated through the use of certification, which guarantees the FT minimum price, an FT premium, as well as pre-financing facilities for small producers in the framework of the contracts that bind them to FT licensees. At the same time, it signals to consumers that stakeholders complied with a number of standards. To complete the model, protagonists of the movement rely on the complicity of consumers to guarantee outlets to producers of the South and, indirectly, to bend the arm of large distribution and agrifood giants.

Therefore, Fair Trade does not position itself in a logic of antinomy towards the free market. Its protagonists firmly believe in its virtues of coordination, or even emancipation, of the individual. Their only problem lies with the fact that the free market is not necessarily at the service of the poor. This is the reason why we must correct its 'imperfections' by bringing it to produce so-called 'pro-poor' results. This endeavour to redeem the market is explicitly backed by the two co-founders of Fairtrade:

Fair Trade operates on the free market and accepts its rules: the price of a product is set based on factors such as efficiency, competition and the quality of the product.... The Fair Trade movement does not challenge market economy in itself. On the other hand, it expects something positive; it seeks to fundamentally rectify its secondary effects in order to come up with completely different social implications. (Roozen and van der Hoff, 2002: 239)

However, by accepting the rules of the free market, Fair Trade protagonists ended up finding themselves caught in contradictions whose exact scale they have still not fully grasped. We can even argue that this pro-market logic leads to a perpetuation of what Karl Marx described as the 'fetishism' attached to commodities (Marx, 1887 [1867]).

According to Marx, under the capitalist mode of production, social relations become apparent, namely through the medium of money, as relations between things. For example, consumers buying a product in a supermarket usually ignore both the manner in which it was produced and the social processes that brought it to the shelves. They therefore tend to be under the impression that commodities have an inherent value and this hides the false objectivity of the price system. Yet, according to Marx, the price system is a product of class relations that tend to be hidden within daily exchanges:[3]

Value, therefore, does not stalk about with a label describing what it is. It is value, rather, that converts every product into a social hieroglyphic. Later on, we try to decipher the hieroglyphic, to get behind the secret of our own social products; for to stamp an object of utility as a value, is just as much a social product as language. (Marx, 1887 [1867]: ch. 1.4)

Approaches such as Fair Trade aim to make social relations along value chains more transparent and to shorten the distance between the upstream (producers in the South) and the downstream (consumers in the North).

However, in the case of Fair Trade, the struggle against the 'anonymity' of the market paradoxically leads to substituting the decried fetishism with a new one. In spite of their progressivist rhetoric, its protagonists are deeply attached to the market price system. Their only objection is to argue that we need an entry price that covers production costs. As we shall see, every aspect of the calculation of the FT minimum price betrays this commodity fetishism: labour power is considered as another '*input*' with an inherent value that can be objectively determined; the argument also maintains that producers should be efficient and adapt to the 'true prices' of the market. Given that 'ethical' consumers ignore these assumptions of the FT economic model, they tend to believe, wrongly, that Fair Trade challenges or subverts the existing price system; this false belief feeds on the mystifying shroud of marketing communication and is the basis of a new form of fetishism.

This section discusses the contradictions of this market redemption attempt, as well as the limitations of the FT mechanism for setting a minimum price, the keystone of Fair Trade.

Fallacies around efficiency

When a theory is filled with contradictions, these generally take the form of 'residual categories', in other words notions or concepts that are inconsistent *a priori*, or even contradictory, in relation to its fundamental axioms (Alexander, 1987). The notion of 'efficiency' enjoys such a status in the paradigm of 'sustainable social economy' in its FT version. Indeed, in the book written by the two co-founders of Fairtrade, numerous sections advocate in favour of the increased efficiency of producers in the South. For instance, one can read:

> Fair Trade should suggest a market structure that reduces transaction costs as much as possible. Inefficiency leads to higher costs, and therefore, loss of markets. (Roozen and van der Hoff, 2002: 245)

> Fair Trade does not encourage inefficient production by suggesting a protected market. (Roozen and van der Hoff, 2002: 247)

Or again:

> Fair Trade is full-fledged trade and must therefore adapt to the key components of the market as a whole: efficiency and quality, financial

flexibility and the use of appropriate techniques are the guarantees of an environmentally sound production model and of long-term economic policy. It therefore implies economically efficient production and marketing in order to be competitive, operate according to the rules of the market and represent good value for money. (van der Hoff, 2005: 37)

This push for economic efficiency is problematic in many respects. It fully illustrates the individualistic approach (as opposed to a holistic approach) of the FT economic model and its unfaltering support of the free market's 'true price' religion. To begin with, one should say that Fair Trade protagonists justify the logic of calculating a cost of sustainable production in terms of the need to take into account the 'hidden' social and environmental costs. By definition, this consists in revaluing upwards the cost 'displayed' by the market for a given product. It is rather odd, therefore, when they argue that the costs of production must be 'efficient'. The question we can ask is the following: where will the economies be made?

Reducing the costs of the factors of production (*inputs*, labour, capital, etc.) could spring to mind. But this is in all likelihood only possible if FT producers pay 'unfair' and 'unsustainable' prices to the rest of the economy, or if a significant growth in global productivity occurs in the nations in question. However, the first assumption is not acceptable for a movement concerned with sustainable working conditions, whereas the second is simply a parameter beyond the scope of the movement.

The second answer consists in reducing transaction costs. Here again there are macroeconomic and institutional considerations that curb the determination and the margin for manoeuvre of producer organisations. Indeed, the level of transaction costs is influenced by the economic development level reached by countries. Generally speaking, they are higher among poor countries than among rich ones (World Bank, 2010b and its *Logistics Performance Index*).

The third answer is that cost reduction can finally refer to achieving economies of scale in production (improving technical efficiency as opposed to allocative efficiency). When production increases, the average cost tends to drop under the effect of economies of scale. In many circumstances, this strategy can no doubt be recommended to producers of the South. But it leaves many questions unanswered: Who will finance the initial additional costs? Where will the production surplus be sold and at what price? What of those who are too poor to expect to reach a certain scale of production?

In fact, the diktat of efficiency is contradictory when it is extended to producers as a whole. On an individual level, one can understand that some groups are more 'efficient' than others, in the sense that they have lower production costs. However, the recommendation that all FT producers should seek to compress their costs in the name of efficiency is problematic, as 'efficiency' in this sense is a relative notion. Producers are 'efficient' vis-à-vis one another. They cannot all be 'efficient' at once. Although this statement may be taken for granted, the issue remains: what is the implication of the efficiency diktat? Without a doubt, it means that the costs of production must not be so prohibitive that FT products cannot find buyers.

At any rate, a mechanical relationship between 'efficiency' and 'price competitiveness' is assumed. Yet, many social determinants come into play in order to loosen the link between these two aspects: exchange rates, tariff and non-tariff barriers, etc. Some producer groups can be 'inefficient' from the point of view of 'production' while being 'competitive' from the point of view of price, and vice versa. A 'lazy' state may for instance manipulate its exchange rate in order to inject 'artificial' price competitiveness into domestic products that would probably not be available on the international market without these distortions. For example, the United States is less 'efficient' than many developing countries for products such as cotton or sugar. Thanks to its subsidies and to the size of its production however, it continues to determine international prices for these products.

Beyond this, we must also point out that the definition of efficiency, or of quality, is a matter of power relations. In the framework of agricultural value chains, the costs saved in the South often create rents in the North. In these circumstances, the high business margins cleared by intermediaries are to some extent a counterpart to the deficit in the negotiating powers of producers in the South. In all these cases, saying that countries of the South must further compress their costs amounts to a contradiction, as their costs of production are already 'efficient'.

Finally, there is the issue of nations that are heavily dependent on the export of basic products and that are 'structurally' inefficient due to geographical disadvantages and problems of scale linked to the small size of their markets and of their production. In spite of cost-reduction efforts, these nations cannot compete with others on the international market. As far as the banana sector is concerned, this is the situation for instance of Caribbean island economies, such as those of Grenada, Saint Lucia, Dominica, and Saint Vincent and the Grenadines (FAO, 2006; Myers, 2004). In such circumstances, considerations of social justice can justify the establishment of trade agreements enabling these nations to access the market under preferential conditions. By insisting on the diktat of efficiency, one would not encourage the inclusion of these cases for which access to 'protected' markets is crucial.

To conclude on this point, let us underscore that Fair Trade protagonists are not prepared to take on all the consequences implied by their rhetoric on efficiency. A symbol of this ambivalence is that the founders of Fairtrade feel that producer organisations must sometimes privilege their own interests and do away with the inefficiencies and bureaucratic red tape of FT certification.[4] On the other hand, and this is where the paradox lies, they are outraged at the arrival of new competitors with the excuse that what they offer to producer organisations is not 'sustainable'.[5] Whatever the case may be, the genuine question is the following: is Fair Trade a 'sustainable' strategy for developing countries? As we shall see in the discussion of the FT minimum price, among others issues, there are reasons to be very sceptical.

The setting of the cost of sustainable production

The setting of the guaranteed minimum price starts with a calculation of the 'cost of sustainable production'. On the basis of a given production standard, this cost is determined by adding up standard production costs and those linked to a 'decent' job as well as the cost of using more environmentally friendly production techniques. For Fair Trade protagonists, the inclusion of these 'hidden' costs is crucial as these are the two main items where economies are made by buyers who are not concerned with an ethical approach. When described in this way, the calculation of the cost of sustainable production seems completely transparent (see Box 4.1).[6]

In reality, things are much more complex. The main difficulty is that the FT economic model is based on the assumption that market prices reflect the 'real' input prices. Thus all inputs that come into play in the calculation of a cost of sustainable production are assessed on the basis of the market prices. This raises the following question: if the market is 'true' on the costs of *inputs*, why argue that the international prices of primary products are not fair? Fairtrade protagonists will answer that it is because there are probably forgotten costs (environment, family labour, etc.) or inadequately assessed costs. Their argument is therefore to invite market actors to be more 'consistent': if there are costs and if these are known to everyone, they should be included in the calculation. This implies that this solidarity approach accepts market assessment standards *a priori*, provided a few 'omissions' are taken into account.

Box 4.1 Method for calculating the cost of
sustainable production and the FT minimum price

The cost of sustainable production varies depending on the reference market (base product, processed product), the type of product (conventional or organic), the average yield per hectare and the rate of exchange of the local currency in US dollars. There exist seven cost items (see Table 4.1).

For each one, costs are estimated by assessing the monetary value of the factors of production involved: (1) labour, (2) inputs and services and (3) investments and capital injected. Evaluation takes into account the depreciation of materials and infrastructures used, taxes, insurance costs, spending for maintenance/repairs, etc. Additional costs are included in item 6 (costs of certification) and 7 (transport, insurance, other taxes, other costs). These various costs are calculated per hectare and per metric ton. The FT minimum price can be calculated at 'farm gate' or FOB (free on board price, i.e. including all costs up to the port of embarkation) depending on whether producer organisations are taking charge or not of transporting their production up to the port of embarkation.

Source: FLO (2010a).

Table 4.1 Type of costs entering into the calculation of the FT minimum price

Rubrics	Costs per hectare	Cost per metric ton
Cost of sustainable production = 1 + 2 + 3 + 4 + 5 + 6		
1. Establishment costs (land preparation, planting trees, facilities, etc.)		
2. Field operation costs (irrigation, fertilisers, seeds, pesticides, herbicides, etc.)		
3. Harvest and post-harvest costs		
4. Transformation and/or processing costs (if applicable)		
5. Product preparation and/or packaging costs (if applicable)		
6. Central structure costs (costs of umbrella organisation)		
Farm gate price = cost of sustainable production + business margin		
7. Export costs (if applicable)		
FOB price = farm gate price + export costs		

This mode of calculation of the cost of sustainable production is, however, a contradiction in terms and anything but 'consistent'. To realise it, one simply ought to see that what amounts to a cost for a group represents an income for another. For example, the price of a cocoa bean is an income for producers, while it is a cost for processing industries. Likewise, by purchasing *inputs*, producers in the South transfer an income to their suppliers and to the employees of the latter. The mode of calculation of the cost of sustainable production seems to assume that all the *inputs* used by producers are purchased at conditions that include no form of exploitation. Yet it is quite likely that these would be much more expensive if they were based on an assessment that takes into account the 'cost of sustainable production' for each of them. For instance, if producers have affordable seeds because their suppliers exploit their employees, it is not justified to consider the market price as the real ('sustainable') price of seeds. In this case, the market price crystallises specific relations of domination. In other words, inconsistency in the mode of calculation of the cost of sustainable production consists in assuming that the price received by producers is 'unfair', but that the prices they pay to the rest of the economy are 'fair', or even unproblematic.

To remain consistent, the Fair Trade approach should also calculate the cost of sustainable production for each input used by producers. As each of these inputs must have been obtained by resorting to other inputs, however, the cost of sustainable production for each of these must be calculated and so on and so forth. This regression *ad infinitum* is not a solution however, as it leads to indetermination. A possible solution is that of a society where all set prices factor in the cost of decent job and that of a sustainable environment. In all logic, the basis for the calculation of any cost of sustainable production should be the setting of a 'sustainable minimum income' at the national level. Without this institutional standard, there is no point in speaking about a cost of sustainable production, as what may be considered as sustainable for a group may not be so for a nation or for the universe as a whole.

This being said, Fair Trade protagonists can simply justify this inconsistency by arguing that producers are 'price takers': they just pay the price of their *inputs*, which they have no control over. This is quite plausible. In such a case, it would also be right to qualify the scope of the cost of sustainable production by specifying that it does apply to certified groups only and that it in no way represents the cost of sustainable production on a national scale. In reality, as we shall see, factoring in this cost of sustainable production in no way guarantees a 'sustainable' way of life for FT-certified producers.

Factoring in family labour

When calculating the cost of sustainable production, the wage that prevails on the 'local market' is the reference price used to determine the cost of family labour and that of temporary hired labour.[7] This presupposes that the market wage is a 'fair' price for this category of workers.

We must first point out that in rural contexts, the notion of 'labour market' is not always straightforward. Wage employment possibilities may be limited due to a fairly equal distribution of land assets and because of the cycle of rural production (the seasonal factor), the low resources of producers and the fact that they resort more willingly to family labour, which is not necessarily easy to substitute with hired labour. In such circumstances, the market wage is not representative of the average remuneration paid to workers. Those who receive it are those with no access to land nor to means of agricultural production.

Besides, even if it is determined, the local market wage can seldom be considered a decent wage. If small producers are as poor as we are told, what of their employees? One may be surprised that the market wage, especially in rural areas, is considered as a suitable indicator of adequate labour force remuneration by an approach concerned with sustainably improving the working conditions of producers and their families.

Choosing to assess the cost of family labour on the basis of the market wage clearly shows, albeit probably unconsciously, the influence of the neoclassical labour supply approach. According to its basic model, workers would only agree to offer their labour on the market when the wage offered to them is higher than their 'reservation wage'. According to Sharif (2000), this approach cannot account for the behaviour of poor workers, generally working extremely long hours and performing physically demanding tasks without being able to meet their basic food needs. He quotes research demonstrating that the poor in developing countries work on average ten to eleven hours every day of the week. Most of them are in a situation of 'distress sale' to quote the phrase used by Kalpana Bardhan (1977). At such low wage levels, they are forced to provide a significant volume of work in order to obtain a certain subsistence income. When their wages rise however, they reduce their labour supply to more physically acceptable levels.

According to Sharif, the neoclassical approach is based on two 'fallacies'. The first is its implicit assumption that the living standard for the poorest households corresponds to the subsistence level of society at large. According to him, such an assumption denies not only the possibility that absolute poverty exists, it also amounts to saying that there is no labour supply below this threshold of subsistence.

The second relates to the assumption according to which the poor have a 'reservation wage'. According to Sharif, workers who have a reservation wage are those who can receive non-wage income that shields them from poverty. As a general rule, this is not the case for the poor, especially in the context of developing countries where few workers benefit from social safety nets. Contrary to non-poor workers, for whom labour supply is null below the reservation wage, poor workers compensate for the decrease of the wage they expect to receive on the market with an increase in the number of hours worked. According to Sharif, what could be considered as the reservation wage of the poor is the 'minimum wage rate at which the quantity of labour supplied by the worker reaches the maximum limit of his/her physical tolerance', which is clearly a very different notion.

To sum up, the calculation of the 'sustainable cost' of family labour and of locally hired labour is not always based on a representative reference of the average labour force remuneration noted in a given region. Assuming that this is the case, it is very unlikely that this price represents a decent wage remuneration for the labour force. This is a contradiction for an approach that is supposed to promote 'sustainable' working conditions.

The determination of the guaranteed minimum price

The guaranteed minimum price is determined once the cost of sustainable production is known. In principle, it amounts to the cost of sustainable production to which a *business margin* is added. The FLO (2010a) methodological document provides no reference as to how this business margin is determined. In the illustrative examples provided, the guaranteed minimum price is arrived at after a 15 per cent business margin is added to the cost of sustainable production. Does this imply that this is the FLO institutional standard? The document provides no clarification. If this is the case, the question we may ask is why not 20 per cent, 50 per cent, etc.?

In practice, the determination of the FT minimum price is slightly more complex. FLO provides three alternative price-setting methods. The use of one or the other is often determined by practical constraints (FLO, 2010b). The first is the *full research* method. This has somewhat been the basis for this discussion thus far, as it is in principle the most 'thorough' method for assessing the cost of sustainable production: the various costs are combed through using detailed empirical data and surveys on the prices of various factors of production. However, the main drawback of this method is that it is costly and time-consuming, sometimes requiring a process of many years; hence the resort to the two following alternatives.

The *easy entrance procedure* is generally used for minor products, namely those belonging to the 'fruit and vegetables' or 'herbs and spices' categories. It is based on already existing standards. The FT minimum price offered is obtained by applying a 'default' percentage of 15 per cent to the average price received by producers the year before its introduction. The third modality is a price extension procedure. Already existing prices based on *comprehensive research* are adjusted in order to come up with new prices (guaranteed minimum price and FT premium). This approach applies to geographical price extensions (example the FT minimum price of an FT product in a given area is used to determine its price in another), extensions based on the difference between the organic and the conventional (example the FT minimum price for a product is used as a starting point to deduce the FT minimum price of an organic product and vice versa), and extensions based on the differences between the farm-gate price and the FOB price (for example, the FT minimum price at the boarding port is deduced on the basis of the farm-gate price and vice versa). Beyond this, it may happen that a single FT minimum price applies everywhere for a product of a given quality, whatever the geographic area.

We should point out that the methods for setting the FT minimum price and the FT premium – with the exception of the comprehensive research method – are *ad hoc*. They help reduce practical problems and gain time. But it can never be argued that FT prices thus obtained actually reflect the true costs of sustainable production (in the sense defined by FLO) in the contexts in which they were assessed. There is no guarantee either that this type of adjustment leads to the setting of a decent price for producers.

In theory, three components can be used in the calculation of a 'sustainable price' for producers: the cost of making the product available (the cost of sustainable production), the average margin that goes to producers under normal circumstances and an additional income transferred by consumers in the North as part of a solidarity approach (such as the FT premium). In principle, Fair Trade provides additional income when it increases the net income of producers and provides a premium to the organisations these belong to. Indeed, as entering the system initially involves higher production costs, it is normal that producers should be compensated for these additional costs. Likewise, the increase in production costs should not lead to a decrease in the net income of FT producers. Under normal circumstances (where market prices do not fall below the production cost for instance), these should receive a net income at least equal to comparable non-FT producers. Otherwise, the system would present no advantage from the point of view of producers taken individually.

This being said, we must acknowledge that the FT system does not actually remove asymmetries between producers and buyers. Producer organisations are for the most part 'price takers'. In spite of the guarantee of a minimum price, the FT system does not generally offer producers the possibility to decide for themselves the price that would enable them to lead a decent life and be free from poverty. This is the case because this economic model faces a dilemma: to improve the living conditions of producers, the minimum price must be fairly high; yet for FT products to find buyers, it is imperative that their prices remain within 'reasonable' limits. This tension probably justifies the opacity around the setting of producer business margins. It also explains the other 'forgotten costs' of the FT minimum price.

The FT minimum price forgets that producers are also consumers

In its current form, the FT economic model considers producers in the South essentially as small businesses. This explains why the cost of sustainable production only includes production-related costs. The consumption expenditures of producers are omitted. In principle, this exclusion is not problematic provided that the consumption needs of producers and their families are taken into account in the business margin that they apply to the cost of sustainable production. The problem, as we have seen, is that the value of this business margin and the logic of its determination are unknown. What is certain on the other hand is that it should not be so high as to risk harming the price competitiveness of FT products. Hence the FT minimum price may seem advantageous in light of the usual conditions of the market and at the same time be insufficient compared with the minimum required for producers to cross the poverty threshold. As one of the co-founders of Fairtrade points out:

> We recently calculated that the income of small coffee producers in Chayotepec and other villages now amounts to around $2 per day. This is a significant improvement compared with the 80 cents from before the creation of UCIRI (Union of Indigenous Communities of the Isthmus Region). Yet, with this low daily wage, small coffee producers are still far from the minimum wage of $3.30 applied in Mexico. Coffee alone is not enough for farmers of the Juarez Mountains to make a decent living. (Roozen and van der Hoff, 2002: 97)

In a proactive poverty reduction logic, the business margin applied on the cost of sustainable production should at least be equal to the *minimum income* that would enable producers and their families to access a basket of essential goods (food, clothing, etc.) and services (children's education, etc.). It is obvious that the main disadvantage of this approach is that FT products might not find any buyers on the market due to their high price. But such is the price that would need to be paid in order to fight against poverty in a voluntaristic way.

This 'more generous' approach of taking basic needs into account, however, is not sufficient. The situation for producers would no doubt improve if the minimum FT price was determined in this way. But they would still be no less vulnerable due to the fact that access to this income would again depend on lasting access to FT markets. Effectively fighting against poverty requires a certain degree of 'decommodification' of labour power, to quote Esping-Andersen (1990). However, within the FT system, the economic prospects for producers depend on the status of their labour power considered as a commodity. For instance, if they have a bad year (caused by exogenous shocks), they are unable to sell and will receive none of the promised benefits. This is due to the fact that the FT system does not provide for social safety nets. One might assume that the FT premium plays this role. This is not the case, however, as the overall amount of the FT premium received by producer organisations is determined by the quantity of FT products sold. Not to mention also that there can be long delays between the sale of FT products and receiving of the FT premium.

In other words, in order to effectively fight against poverty, social safety nets must be established so as to *smooth over* the consumption of producers and their families, and to ensure that these are increasingly autonomous vis-à-vis production cycle hazards. Free market logic is less harmful to the poor when these social insurance mechanisms become institutionalised. In their absence, market access for the poorest becomes more problematic. The principle of social insurance is actually one of the premises of the general equilibrium theory. In order to demonstrate the allocative efficiency of the market, the theory assumes, among other things, that individuals receive 'initial endowments' that will enable them to live comfortably without needing to trade their whole lives through (Guerrien, 1999: 65–6). From an empirical point of view, studies have shown that nations actively involved in globalisation tend to have a very broad public sector (measured in terms of the public expenditure/ GDP ratio). The following explanation is provided: in countries heavily exposed to international trade, the government plays an important role in terms of risk reduction (Mayda et al., 2007; Rodrik, 1998).

If developing countries themselves do not have the means to establish these social safety nets in favour of their populations, it would be unreasonable to expect this from Fair Trade; yet it is worth noting this, if only to demonstrate the limits of its approach. This being said, a *second best* solution and one that is less demanding could be, for instance, to encourage economic diversification and the achievement of the food sovereignty objective. In the absence of social safety nets, this initiative would at least enable producers and their families to possibly enjoy several sources of income and to reduce their food dependency. In the FT approach, these objectives are considered as secondary. Even though their importance may be recognised, they remain subordinate to the export of products in demand by the market. In principle, the FT system boosts economic diversification if the income effect – financial gains collected, freeing up time and inputs for other forms of production – is higher than the substitution effect (the income increase from Fairtrade leads to specialisation in FT products and the phasing out of other production).

Uncertainties and Asymmetries of the FT Economic Model

As we have just seen, the FT minimum price does not necessarily enable producers to move out of poverty due to the way it is calculated and to the imperative of price competitiveness. This does not immediately imply that the FT economic model is unable to play its income stabilisation role. If FT prices cannot be 'generous', one can assume that they can theoretically fulfil this function. However, if we take into account the other element in the equation, namely market access, it would seem that Fair Trade does not fulfil its stabilisation and income increase promises except under very specific circumstances.

Fair Trade is based on free trade logic

Contrary to what one might think, the FT economic model does not necessarily remove price uncertainty, in other words, that which it was designed to prevent. First of all, there is the fact that the minimum price and the premium are nominal prices. Therefore, they are sensitive to the evolution of exchange rates and inflation.

The FT prices and premiums are initially calculated in local currency, and then expressed in foreign currency (namely dollars and euros). For countries that do not have a fixed parity with these currencies, the exchange rate risk is not removed by the FT economic model: in case of foreign currency appreciation (for example when dollars are exchanged against more local currency), producers receive an amount which is higher in local currency than what they should have received, and vice versa in case of a depreciation. Due to these wealth effects, it may be – depending on the provisions stipulated in the contracts – that the guaranteed minimum price expressed in local currency is lower in some cases than the original reference price calculated in the local currency.

Not taking into account inflation is also problematic. Depending on time lags between updates, FT prices can remain fixed over a period whose duration may vary. Yet inflation is a crucial aspect of the fight against poverty. It affects production overheads: the price of some inputs can increase, therefore adding to the costs of production. It also has an impact on the purchasing power of producers and on the internal terms of trade (between rural producers and urban dwellers). To take the case of coffee, the Fair Trade flagship product, it would seem that the guaranteed minimum price lost 41 per cent of its real value between 1988 and 2008 (Bacon, 2010).[8]

It would seem that the FT prices and premiums are now updated every two years to take into account the evolution of inflation and exchange rates. As for inflation, FLO refers to the consumer price index (CPI) prevalent in the relevant countries. However, it remains to be seen if a specific adjustment is planned for agricultural producers, as the national CPI is generally not a good indicator of the evolution of the standard of living in rural areas. A comprehensive review of all prices should normally take place every eight years at the most (FLO, 2010b).

The most fundamental limit of the FT economic model is that it does not guarantee that the available FT production will entirely be sold at FT conditions. This raises the following question: what point is there in guaranteeing a minimum price if there is no matching commitment in terms of market access? This cannot be explained by the difficulty inherent in making forecasts in contexts where production is liable to numerous risks. Given that the calculation of the FT minimum price is based on the average agricultural productivity recorded in specific areas, one should logically expect that FT producers have the possibility to sell a volume that would at least enable them to recover their costs on FT markets. But FT producers have no such guarantee *a priori*. In other words, securing FT certification does not equate to a promise of access to FT markets. Labelling initiatives should no doubt seek to develop FT markets and act as intermediaries between buyers and producers. However, the guarantee for outlets is not included in the contract that binds them to FT producers.

What we must understand clearly is that FLO simply defines the rules of the game for FT markets (certification, minimum price, premium, pre-financing, traceability, etc.). It does not play any part in the FT market operations.[9] This has three implications. In principle, there is no trading below the FT minimum price on FT markets. Second, securing a higher price is dependent upon the outcome of negotiations between producers and their clients. This implies that there is no reason *a priori* for the latter to pay higher prices than the FT minimum. Finally, FT licensees independently decide the distribution of their purchases – in other words which groups they will buy from. Likewise, producers must mobilise their resources and 'social capital' in order to find FT markets themselves. Some will be able to access FT markets on a regular basis while others will find it more difficult. This means that in the FT system, prices and market access are determined on the basis of competition. This justifies the relevance of studying who enters the FT system and under what conditions. We should be grateful to Sushil Mohan (2010) for being one of the rare authors to have understood that Fair Trade is a logical continuation of free trade and not an alternative to it:

It is wrong to consider Fair Trade as a development of a market that is different from the 'free market'. All that is happening is that Fair Trade opens up an alternative speciality trading channel within the free market. The market fundamentals, the demand, supply and market competitiveness conditions for Fair Trade products, follow conventional trade practices. Fair Trade works not because it subsidises goods no one wants, but because some free market consumers are willing to support it. Whether they are 'objectively' right to do so is important but irrelevant to this particular line of argument – Fair Trade fulfils a subjective preference. Fair Trade products have to compete in the market just like any other speciality market product. Fair Trade producers can receive the Fair Trade prices and premiums only if they have a buyer willing to pay them. Therefore Fair Trade does not pose any challenge to the free market system; rather it is a part of that system that increases the welfare of a target group through a speciality market. (Mohan, 2010: 45–6)

These considerations explain how the average price (Total revenue/ Total volume sold) received by FT producers can sometimes be lower than the guaranteed FT minimum price. For example, if only part of the production is actually sold at FT conditions, it follows that the remainder is sold at actual market prices in the best of cases. If the market price is lower than the FT price, this can be construed as a form of 'dumping' in so far as part of the FT production is likely sold at a price that does not reflect the cost of sustainable production incurred. Obviously, setting a minimum price does not help to reduce price uncertainty, except if it is based on actual market promises.

The FT contract: reflections on the uncertainties of a promise

On this last point, it should be pointed out that labelling initiatives add a degree of mystification. In their communications, they underscore the guarantee of an FT minimum price that covers the costs of production. Evidence of this is that it is not rare to find publications that present charts on the compared evolution of the FT price and the market price. This information is always presented in the same way: by construction, the FT price evolution curve is always above that of the market price or on the same level (for episodes where the latter is higher than the FT minimum price *ex ante*).[10] This type of graphical argument actually contributes to increasing the attractiveness of Fair Trade.

These types of charts, however, amount more to a marketing ploy than to serious economic analysis, as they contain two conjectures.[11] The first fallacious conjecture is that the *ex ante* guaranteed price is *always* lower than or equal to the average price received *ex post* by FT producers. This implies that the income of FT producers is *very* stable and tends to increase. This assumption is only valid if the FT production volume sold at FT conditions is high for every year of the period in consideration. The second fallacious conjecture is that the *ex ante* guaranteed price is adjusted upwards to market price level when the latter is higher. This assumption is only valid if the adjustment is included in contract clauses that bind FT producers and their clients and/or if FT producers have the possibility to sell their FT production at market price. In other words, the problem with this kind of presentation is that it is not clear whether it describes the theoretical stabilisation function of the FT price or the empirical impact of Fair Trade over a given period.

In all cases, these types of analysis fail to point out that (1) the FT minimum price is guaranteed only for production volume sold on FT markets, (2) the FT production volume is rarely sold 100 per cent on FT markets, and (3) FT producers have higher average costs, all other things being equal. When these considerations are taken into account, it follows that Fair Trade does not *necessarily* help to stabilise income and/or to reduce rural poverty. In certain circumstances, it can even make the situation worse for producers.

To assess the impact of Fair Trade on the income of producers (those selling products certified FT),[12] two aspects can be looked at:

- the absolute impact on gross income and net income (gross income minus overall costs),
- the net impact: the differential impact of Fair Trade (net income of FT producers vs net income of a comparable group of non-FT producers).

From our point of view, a more heuristic approach would consist in focusing on the second aspect, as what matters after all is to know how much producers obtain from investing resources in one activity rather than another. Indeed, higher gross income for FT producers does not reveal the net impact of Fair Trade. In principle, given that they generally have higher production costs, one might expect that they should receive higher prices. It is possible that FT producers have a higher gross income and a lower net income simultaneously. To assess the net impact of Fair Trade, one must focus on the differential margin that can be achieved through it. In other words, the unit margin (example a profit of €X per kilo of coffee) collected by FT producers is compared to that obtained by non-FT producers. All things being equal, if the net gains (outstanding gains once production costs have been deducted) for each unit of a product sold are higher for the former, then we can argue that Fair Trade has had a positive impact; in the opposite case, the impact is negative.

This assessment is made more complex, however, by uncertainties regarding FT outlets. As FT producers do not sell their entire production on FT markets, they tend to sell the remainder at the market price. Yet this can take on extreme values: it can be lower than the conventional production cost as it can be higher than the FT minimum price (which in turn can be higher than the conventional production cost). It can also lie anywhere between these two values. In other words, the net local impact is influenced by (1) differences between unit margins, (2) their degree of specialisation (the share of the overall production sold on the FT market) and (3) the evolution of agricultural productivity. On the basis of realistic assumptions, we can easily arrive at the following results for two initially comparable groups:[13]

- When the market unit margin is higher than the FT unit margin, the net income of non-FT producers is higher than that of FT producers selling at FT price. For the latter, the opportunity cost is all the greater if the volume sold on the FT market is significant. In such circumstances, FT certification opportunity costs can be high if FT price readjustment mechanisms are not provided for.
- When the market unit margin is equal to the FT unit margin, net income in both cases is equal. FT producers however have the advantage of receiving the premium on top.
- When the market unit margin is lower than the FT unit margin, different scenarios may be envisaged.[14] But one conclusion remains: the net impact of Fair Trade is only demonstrated when FT sales are high and/or when the unit margin differential is significant. Even in these circumstances, there is no guarantee either that the net income of FT producers will be positive. For instance, in cases where market rates are very low (below the conventional production cost), FT producers who did not have a significant access to FT markets will

have a net income that is negative and lower than that of non-FT producers.

These results are mostly valid in the short term (where it is reasonable to assume that agricultural productivity does not change much). In the medium and long term, however, the induced effects should also be taken into account, namely the influence of Fair Trade on the evolution of agricultural productivity and on the allocation of factors of production (if it leads to increased specialisation or to diversification).

At any rate, it is clear that Fair Trade only fully plays its role of income stabilisation when FT production volume sold under FT conditions is significant. Besides, it only contributes to poverty reduction when FT prices are set at rather high levels and if it induces a growth in productivity. Hence our conclusion: all things being equal, the local impact of Fair Trade depends on the contractual provisions that bind FT producers to FT buyers. This will be all the more important if (1) the FT unit margin is high and generally higher than the market unit margin and if (2) the purchase commitments tend to apply to 100 per cent of the FT production every year.[15] Therefore, to study the local impact of Fair Trade, one must look at the extent to which the promises made by each and everyone were kept or not, rather than relying only on charts showing the comparative evolution between the FT minimum price and the market price, or general statements on gross income that is higher for FT producers, or even the higher prices that they receive.

Fair Trade does not rub out North–South asymmetries

As we have just seen, the FT economic model does not necessarily reduce uncertainties – in terms of prices, exchange rates and market access – that producers in the South are facing. Holding FT certification in no way guarantees higher income for producers in the South. Like any investment, it is a gamble on the future. The Fair Trade promise is neither more nor less risky than other types of investments, as it inevitably relies on market logic. As has been underscored by numerous authors, the Fair Trade paradox is that it attempts to transform the market while borrowing its structures. As a result, the FT system exhibits asymmetries usually seen in international trade:

- Asymmetries between consumers in the North and producers in the South: the preferences of consumers in the North determine to some extent the FT price as well as the growth of the FT market. They act out of solidarity, but are not forced to do so. Consumers also have a choice between different FT or 'ethical' products. In contrast, producers are unable to create a competition amongst consumers. On a general level, market growth for 'ethical' or 'sustainable' products is limited by consumption expenditure (namely food) of citizens in the North, which makes up a small part of their budget.

- Asymmetries between producers and traders: producers are 'price takers' – for the most part, they do not have much influence on prices. In addition, they run risks when they choose to specialise in FT products. When FT markets are not found, no compensation is planned for the loss of earnings incurred due to the increase in production costs. In contrast, traders are not bound in terms of the volume of FT products they purchase. They are not bound to purchase FT products either, nor to go beyond the FT minimum price. Finally, they can leave the FT system at any time without incurring significant costs.

- Asymmetries between producers and labelling initiatives: standards are developed by labelling initiatives, and producers can usually change them very little. If their FT products do not sell at the desired volume, or if they do not have the means to renew their certification – precisely because they did not sell a significant volume – producers are left stranded. In other words, faced with the risks of the market, producers have to fend for themselves. In such circumstances, labelling initiatives can only 'advise' them or 'sensitise' their partners so they buy more. Besides, labelling initiatives are free to modify the costs of certification as well as the licensing tariffs. When this happens, such prices tend to be pushed upwards.

- Asymmetries between consumers and distribution networks: Fair Trade entered into supermarkets, not because of a demand from consumers but because distribution networks accepted this bet. In other words, consumers are 'product takers'. Distribution networks themselves determine which products can be accessed by consumers. In fact, regardless of the degree of generosity of the latter, the growth of FT markets is based in the last instance on the policy of distribution networks.

In addition to maintaining these asymmetries, there is also a convergence of interests between national labelling initiatives and companies that may apply for the FT licence. We must not simply assume that labelling initiatives are here only for the 'good' of poor small producers. They certainly attempt to defend a certain vision of the world. Beyond their original mission, they have become bureaucracies in need of economic resources in order to survive in an environment where their legitimacy, as well as their position in the area of 'ethical' trade, is increasingly threatened by competing approaches. Whatever the case might be, we are forced to acknowledge that, until recently, the success of FT sales has led to greater financial autonomy for labelling initiatives. Their expenditures are increasingly funded by licensing fees.

Given that the amount of such fees depends on the number of licensees and on the volume of FT products that they commercialise, it is in the interest of labelling initiatives to have an 'attractive' marketing policy towards their clients. This configuration can explain the great power of FT licensees in the process of FT price readjustment, such as those that occurred between the end of 2006 and the beginning of 2007. At that time, as narrated by Bacon (2010), the Latin American and Caribbean Network of Smallholder Fair Trade Producers bumped up against the reluctance of labelling initiatives, and initially those of FLO, when their representatives asked for the FT coffee minimum price to be reassessed upwards. Some participants even went so far as to describe the producers as 'greedy'. Labelling initiatives feared that the proposed price increase would be prohibitive for licensee companies. Yet producers had an important argument to put forward, namely the constant decline of the purchasing power of the FT minimum price since 1988. Besides, some of them felt that the FT minimum price would be unable to compensate the estimated cost of sustainable production. The agreed price ended up being a 'compromise' well below that proposed by the producers. In spite of this, even to get to this point, civil society and alternative trade organisations had to join in the fight alongside the producers.[16]

The relevance of the analysis presented thus far is actually confirmed by the recent boom in the price of agricultural raw materials. Instead of this proving an advantage to FT producers, it would seem that this favourable conjuncture paradoxically led to a disruption of FT value chains. As small FT producers are generally poor and have cash flow difficulties sometimes caused by an increase in the cost of inputs, intermediaries speculating on a price increase short-circuit Fair Trade networks by offering very early to producers, before harvests, a price that is higher than the FT price, but lower than the ultimate anticipated price. As a result of this, producers in the South pull out of FT value chains by not fulfilling their commitments towards the cooperatives to which they belong, a rationale which is easy to understand. It is normal for them to sell to the highest bidder, especially when they can be paid very early and in cash. But as they have little information on market trends, this short-term vision generates a rent to speculators who are better informed. Therefore, although small producers receive a better price than the FT price, they do not benefit from all the price increase observed in the markets.[17] This confirms a previous observation, namely that charts which assume an automatic adjustment of the FT price in relation to the market price when the latter is higher pertain more to marketing than to serious empirical analysis.

This withdrawal of small producers can contribute to slowing down the growth of production sold on FT markets. From the point of view of labelling initiatives, this type of evolution can affect the licensee fees that they receive. Given the competitive approach of other labels, the practices of distribution networks when it comes to setting margins and the economic crisis that has unevenly affected rich countries since 2008, it is not surprising to see that actors formerly specialised in North–South trade have started redeploying their efforts towards North–North Fair Trade.[18] On this point, one is entitled to wonder whether these diversification strategies do not contribute to creating further confusion amongst consumers (should they privilege local producers or foreign producers?) and to hijacking the original mission of Fair Trade, a label that is becoming just another marketing ploy.

Whatever the case, we find ourselves in a strange context where the rise in raw material prices does not favour labelling initiatives. While this situation should benefit producers, it tends to dry up sources of income for Fair Trade organisations. It is no doubt within this perspective that we should analyse the support of labelling initiatives for the G20 project aiming to 'regulate' the price of raw materials.[19] Indeed, if the prices of raw materials continue to rise, Fair Trade might become unable to survive much longer, *mutatis mutandis*. Conversely, if they should decrease, as was the case in the past, the Fair Trade message would remain topical and difficult to ignore. So much so that the interests of small producers and those of Fair Trade do not always match. The former want good prices for their products while the latter would ideally wish for mid-range prices that are not volatile. Needless to say, this is a very peculiar way of fighting poverty.

In the end, we must recognise that the FT system puts producer organisations in a very uncomfortable situation. On the one hand, they cover most of the costs and bear most of the risks. On the other, they have no guarantee of a return on their investments. In contrast, economic intermediaries run no major risk[20] (due to the economic insignificance of the FT market and to the fact that they have a large choice of suppliers) and the profits are almost guaranteed. As far as labelling initiatives are concerned, outside of staff reduction, the main risk relates to issues of reputation. In such conditions, where costs and profits are individualised, it is difficult to talk about reciprocity and solidarity. As we shall see in the remainder of this book, the pro-market logic of Fairtrade led to unexpected and almost unbelievable results, to say the least, both for its protagonists and for its supporters.

The Local Impact of Fair Trade

Fair Trade covers almost all developing countries in its scope of activity. Its implantation has thus far been based on an extensive growth strategy: many countries are covered, but the 'rate of penetration' remains low in each country. In 2009, there was effective certification demand in 60 developing countries. In a little over one out of three of these countries, the number of organisations having received FT certification is no more than six. The implantation of the movement was also very uneven depending on the country: six countries account for 40 per cent of organisations that have received FT certification[20] (see Table 4.2). Consequently, one cannot

Table 4.2   Distribution of FT groups in 2009

	Number of countries covered	% of total countries covered	Number of FT groups	% of total FT groups
Countries with 1 FT group	11	18.3	11	1.3
Between 2 and 5 FT groups	11	18.3	33	4.0
Between 6 and 10 FT groups	14	23.3	104	12.6
Between 11 and 20 FT groups	11	18.3	165	20.0
Between 21 and 40 FT groups	7	11.7	185	22.4
More than 40 FT groups	6	10.0	329	39.8
Total	60	100.0	827	100.0

Source: FLO (2010e).

expect Fair Trade to have nationwide impact. As a general rule, the scope of this impact has been local.

Methodological considerations

What is the local impact of Fair Trade? To what extent did it contribute to changing the living conditions of producers in the South? The rich literature existing on this topic is so heterogeneous – from the point of view of motivations, methodologies used, products and areas covered, etc. – that arguments are found at both extremes of the spectrum. An impartial reader examining these works in order to identify a few key conclusions would end up more confused and disoriented than anything else. This situation is however not specific to Fair Trade. It is frequent in most debates around development economics. From our point of view, the weight of ideology and doctrinal convictions plays a non-trivial role. It is indeed rare to find authors providing arguments that go against the theoretical propositions of the communities that they identify with. But ideology does not explain everything. From our point of view, the biggest source of disappointment in this impact literature is its 'empiricist' and 'a-theoretical' nature.

To demonstrate or deny the alleged impact of Fair Trade, on close inspection it seems that the arguments mobilised have been based on considerations of quantity. To lend clout to their cause, both labelling initiatives and their detractors have tended to quote numerous carefully selected studies, or even to resort to anecdotes. This approach, however, is flawed from a logical point of view, even if it can prove efficient from a media point of view. In epistemology, this is notoriously referred to as the 'problem of induction'. The fact that X number of observations show this or that does not prove anything that would logically give the status of 'law' or irrefutable empirical generality to the phenomenon under scrutiny.

In social science, things are more complicated than in 'hard' science. One cannot dismiss a theoretical proposition by quoting examples where it is refuted. Conversely, one cannot prove the general empirical validity of a theoretical proposition by arguing on the basis of the significant number of works that confirm it. Given the importance of contextual and institutional parameters, a more heuristic approach would consist in determining the conditions of validity of the theoretical proposition, and possibly identifying the causality mechanisms that it puts forward. The problem thus far is that there has been an attempt to assess the impact of Fair Trade without first querying the prerequisites for the validity of its economic model. It is therefore not surprising to note a degree of confusion.

For the most part, the results of this literature on the microeconomic impact are trivial in the sense that they can easily be predicted by theory (the theoretical analysis of the FT economic model). Indeed, it is easy to obtain results for or against Fair Trade. In contexts where market prices are extremely low, Fair Trade tends to have a substantial impact for producer organisations that sold significant volumes (their members have a higher than average income, they are less indebted, the premium is higher, therefore more economic and social investments can be made, etc.). Conversely, where market prices are higher than the FT price, the impact of Fair Trade is less significant. In fact, one might push the logic to its extreme and argue that it is in the interest of Fair Trade protagonists to grant certification to organisations based in areas where market prices are always low, where workers suffer more from exploitation and where social infrastructures are basic. In such circumstances, impact studies would no doubt argue that, in the majority of cases, Fair Trade provides significant advantages; and vice versa for opponents. But in reality, market prices are not always at their lowest and the development level of regions differs depending on the context, as is the case with the social and economic status of workers. This introduces a few additional complexities.

This is to say that the search for the local impact of Fair Trade is often in vain when it is not informed by theory. Fair Trade is not a *deus ex machina* that might land, as if by chance, on a *no man's land*. It selects specific types of producers in contexts that can be more or less accommodating of the causes it seeks to promote. Its local impact cannot be thoroughly addressed without an in-depth study of (1) the processes leading to the selection of FT producer organisations, (2) the respect by all of the FT contract promises (FT minimum price, access to FT markets, pre-financing possibilities, etc.) and (3), the variably accommodating nature of the contexts under consideration. The difficulty with this literature is that it tends to overshadow these key considerations.[21]

Illustrations

Let us illustrate this latter point on the basis of two studies conducted under the initiative of organisations for the promotion of Fair Trade. The first is a literature review which, to my mind, is typical of the types of broad results that it presents. I chose the second publication due to its methodological shift compared with most other works.

First illustration: The Last Ten Years: A Comprehensive Review of the Literature on the Impact of Fairtrade *(Nelson and Pound, 2009)*

This research was commissioned by the Fairtrade Foundation (UK) and it summarises 33 case studies on the local impact of Fair Trade (25 for coffee; 4 for bananas; 3 for cocoa; 1 for fruits and vegetables) distributed as follows: 26 relate to Latin America and the Caribbean, 7 to Africa and none to Asia. Writings in French were not included. Only two studies focus on hired labour organisations. The main results are as follows:

- Fair Trade contributed to an income increase for producers. It also led to a stabilisation of their income. This often encouraged the rooting of poor communities into agriculture.
- There is no clear conclusion on economic diversification: the FT system can encourage it, but it can also promote specialisation.
- There is no clear conclusion either on the impact of Fair Trade from the perspective of quality improvement.
- Compared with their non-FT counterparts, FT producers often have access to pre-financing possibilities as part of their production activities.
- It would seem that geographical marginalisation is a factor that hinders successful involvement in the FT system.
- Fair Trade promotes the development of individual capacity (more self-esteem, better knowledge of export markets, better access to training, better negotiation skills). Nevertheless, producers are not always well informed of the ins and outs of the FT system.
- Fair Trade has positive impacts on the community (development of community life and more established democracy amongst organisations).
- There are very few elements on gender inequalities except that, in the case of coffee, women tend not to be involved. This means that they have limited control over the income generated by Fair Trade. Sometimes, participation in the FT system increases the 'twin burden' borne by women. In some cases, it can foster their emancipation.
- There is very little data on the impact of Fair Trade in the area of environment. However, the adoption of organic production does involve a significant increase in production costs (labour costs namely).

- Very little data on the use and impact of the FT premium is available.
- Very little data on the distribution of income along the FT value chains is available.
- It is to be noted that this document never mentions child labour, even though it states that in some cases, Fair Trade promoted the schooling of the children of FT producers.

From our point of view, the most important outcome of this literature review is its acknowledgement that, for now, existing studies cannot serve as a basis to identify a positive and definite impact of Fair Trade in terms of poverty reduction:

> While those producers selling all or a part of their production to Fairtrade are often better off than their neighbours, and usually more able to cover their basic needs and some modest investments, it is difficult to assess from the studies [quoted] the degree to which participation in Fairtrade is enabling producers to escape poverty. While some studies mention a dramatic improvement in livelihoods, others emphasise that producer families are still only surviving and covering basic needs. Some suggest that Fairtrade needs to be supplemented by other development policies and initiatives to raise rural livelihoods to a more sustainable level. (Nelson and Pound, 2009: 10)

Second illustration: The Impact of Fair Trade *(Ruben, 2009)*

This book, whose results were included in the previous summary document, starts by underscoring the methodological weaknesses of most existing studies, namely that they do not conduct baseline studies, do away with the use of reference groups and do not take into account the possible selection bias involved in participation in the FT system.

> Several studies have tried to capture the impact of Fair Trade for local producers and households, but sound empirical evidence regarding social, economic and ecological impact remains scattered and sometimes contradictory. Due to the notable absence of base-line studies and reference groups, it remains difficult to precisely assess the welfare impact at household and cooperative level. Therefore, a new methodological framework has been developed and applied in this study that permits to capture the tangible and less-tangible effects of Fair Trade involvement. (Ruben, 2009: 19)

Box 4.2 Major approaches in terms of impact studies

In terms of impact study, there are three main types of approach: (1) before/after: FT groups are compared before and after entry into the FT system; (2) FT group (treatment group) vs non-FT group (reference group); (3) double differences, in which the two previous approaches are combined – a before/after analysis (at the time of evaluation) for each group followed by a comparative analysis of the two groups.

A practical difficulty linked with this latter approach is that there is generally a lack of data for the two groups in the period preceding the entry of the treatment group into the FT system. This explains why the articles collected in Ruben (2009) are based on the second approach. Another major difficulty pertains to the fact that the person conducting the evaluation cannot know what would have happened if the treatment group had not entered the FT system (the 'counter-factual question'). A solution would be to use the average values observed for the reference group. This procedure is not suitable, however, as the treatment group may have non-average characteristics (even without being involved in the FT system). In order to reduce potential 'selection biases', a method generally consists in pairing the treatment group with another reference group that is similar in terms of most of its 'pre-treatment' characteristics. The analyst uses the econometric techniques that have been developed for this purpose. In principle, the variables selected to pair up the two groups should influence the decision to enter the FT system, rather than the outcomes linked to FT certification.

This compilation of articles includes case studies on six countries (Peru, Costa Rica, Ecuador, Ghana, Kenya and Mexico) and four products: coffee, handicrafts, herbs and bananas. The methodology used is in line with existing microeconomic standards (see Box 4.2). According to the editor of the book, this publication 'is the first comparative quantitative assessment of the Fair Trade impact on farmers' welfare and attitudes' (Ruben, 2009: 20). The main results are summed up below.[22] It should be pointed out that this book, published with the support of Solidaridad, does not actually address the issue of whether Fair Trade helped lift producers out of poverty.

With regard to production, yields, prices and profits:

- For bananas especially, there is an increase in production, namely the yield per hectare. In the case of coffee, this led to specialisation and the reduction of *inputs* committed to other production.
- Guaranteed markets and stable prices sometimes encourage producers to invest in techniques that increase productivity.

For household income:

- FT producers receive prices that are stable and sometimes high.
- The highest net income and profits are collected by FT producers holding an organic certification (in spite of the higher costs incurred by organic farming). Income differences are slight between producers on the FT market (not organic) and non-FT producers.
- In most observed cases, FT income represents on average 70 to 90 per cent of household income. Fair Trade therefore tends to lead to specialisation and the reduction of economic diversification among organisations that can sell large quantities on FT markets.

With regard to household expenditure:

- Even though there may be differences between FT households and non-FT households in terms of net income, these do not appear at the level of expenditure. On the other hand, it would seem that FT households tend to spend more on long-term investments (education, durable household goods, improving the living conditions of the household, etc.). In other words, FT households are not richer than average, but they invest in areas that will have a positive impact on their welfare in the long term.

Access to credit:

- There is a positive effect for households involved in the FT system: FT contracts seem to play the role of collateral for credit institutions.

Perceptions of welfare and attitudes towards risk:

- There is no inherent effect linked to entering the FT system in terms of perceptions of welfare. It would seem however that, as a general rule, FT producers are more prepared to take risks than non-FT producers.

As we can see through these two illustrations, the impact literature focused essentially on two products (coffee and bananas) and a single region (Latin America).[23] The results presented are generally consistent with one another and are quite plausible. Broadly speaking, these two publications argue that there is a slight improvement for producer organisations that have been fortunate enough to sell, but this impact is all but exceptional: 'Better but not great', to quote the actual title of the Jaffee (2009) article. However, these results should be interpreted with caution due to the 'selection bias' contained in this type of literature.

The selection bias problem

As a general rule, impact studies have been based on the assumption that the implementation of Fair Trade experienced a 100 per cent success rate. To assess its benefits, these studies focused on organisations for which some of the FT promises could be seen to have been fulfilled. This explains why 'failures' were never documented, nor cases where certification was not granted for a number of reasons, nor cases where producer organisations withdrew from the FT system because they saw nothing in it in spite of its promises. This situation may not be frequent in Latin America. In the case of West Africa, I personally witnessed cases of failure: producer organisations that were initially certified withdrew from the FT system because of poor sales and had no means of renewing their certification. Beyond these failures, even for certified organisations, there is scant information on the certification processes, how long they took, difficulties encountered, how long it took before initial benefits were received, etc. This is unfortunate.

The first major question is the following: were producers organised by Fair Trade or was this done well before certification? As a general rule, the poorest producers are inadequately structured and are marginalised. They have no access to information on economic opportunities. Public authorities do not sufficiently take them into account and often they do not have the means to travel or pay the costs of specific administrative procedures. Without outside help, mainly from NGOs or development agencies, poor producers are not easy to organise. There is no guarantee either that they would have the capacity to export large volumes of production. Thus, from the perspective of labelling initiatives, the FT certification process is longer, more costly, riskier and more complex to implement in the case of small producers who are not yet structured in the form of an association or cooperative.[24] This explains why Fair Trade tends to select groups of producers that already have a certain level of organisational capacity as priority targets.

A second major question is the following: where does the certification initiative originate? The certification approach can be initiated by traders (private actors most often; sometimes also parastatal actors) when they receive new orders for FT products. In such cases, FT certification can be speedy, as there is already a history between the traders and the producer groups in question, and because the promise of new FT markets is generally heartily welcomed by labelling initiatives. The certification approach can also be initiated by NGOs or development agencies that separately seek FT markets through their networks of relations. It should be pointed out that Fair Trade has become a new field where NGOs enter with a view to diversify their portfolio of development actions. Labelling initiatives can also initiate certification processes. In most cases, they build on the organisational work carried out by NGOs or by existing marketing structures. As a general rule, certification processes initiated by traders, or by labelling initiatives, have in principle a greater chance of success, as producers are guaranteed stable FT markets where to sell off their products.

As pointed out by Fridell (2007: 220), in the Latin American context, Fair Trade success stories have two main features. They relate to cooperatives that were well organised before entering the FT system and that benefited from 'the long-term presence of an "international interlocutor" who has been essential for gaining access to the fair trade network and developing ties with Northern partners'. The interlocutor in question has taken on many guises: Christian missionaries, agricultural technicians, representatives of Fair Trade organisations, NGOs, development agencies, etc.[25]

The selection bias is the Achilles heel of the literature on the impact of Fair Trade. The results of each study may prove interesting when taken in isolation, but they can in no way be generalised. Due to their individualistic methodology, modern econometric techniques simply cannot correct this selection bias. They certainly enable the pairing of a treatment group with another similar group from the point of view of the characteristics of its members. But this overlooks the fact that this selection borrows from social processes and that the whole is not the sum of its parts. Organisations can be distinguished on the basis of parameters such as their age, geographical location, links with specific groups of influence, etc. These types of consideration mean that two groups that are similar from the point of view of the individual characteristics of their members are not necessarily comparable from the point of view of their 'social capital' or their ability to establish international relationships or influence domestic policy. Evidence of this, as could be illustrated by Ruben (2009), certainly one of the most thorough studies from the point of view of methodology, is that, for the most part, the FT producer organisations selected have somewhat idiosyncratic characteristics.[26]

The deficit of contextualisation

Beyond the selection bias, another difficulty is that most of the studies did not sufficiently detail the extent to which the FT contract was complied with: on average, how much was sold annually? In cases where the whole FT production was not sold, what happened to the remainder? What were the delays before cashing in the premium? What share of the premium was invested in renewing the certification?[27] The lack of detailed information on these types of questions is certainly unfortunate. It leads to global and synthetic analyses that can hide numerous discrepancies from one year to the next. Yet, in circumstances where things do not work well (namely, there are no large FT sales), producers owe their survival and their maintenance within the FT system to their resilience, their resourcefulness and the multifaceted forms of aid that they may receive from partners outside the FT system.

In the same vein, another limitation of this impact literature is that it does not systematically examine the extent to which the specificities of the social and economic context under study facilitated or not the successful implementation of Fair Trade. Without claiming to exhaust the various institutional and contextual parameters, we can mention market structures (credit, labour, exports, land), existing policies (nature and quality of social infrastructures, for example), the nature of specialisation (export agriculture vs subsistence agriculture and economic diversification vs specialisation, for example), price evolution (domestic inflation, prices of goods and services consumed by producers, evolution of international prices of imported goods, for example), class relations (socioeconomic inequalities and so on), etc. Just to take the case of inflation, it is surprising to note the extent of the silence of the impact literature on this. However, producers are twice penalised by it: it increases their costs of production and reduces their purchasing power.

From this point of view, the study by Jaffee (2009) is an interesting exception. In the case of coffee producers based in Oaxaca in Mexico, the FT minimum price seemingly stayed level for ten years, a situation which has become problematic for FT producers, even if their situation was more enviable than that of non-FT producers.[28] Jaffee also demonstrates that in the context of the falling coffee prices at the beginning of the year 2000,

FT producers lost as much money as non-FT producers. In both cases, net household income declined in similar proportions.[29] Nonetheless, due to FT pre-financing mechanisms, FT producers were less in debt than non-FT producers and were less dependent upon external funding.

Conclusion

To close this discussion, we could say that Fair Trade has a slight impact for producer associations or cooperatives that have significant organisational predispositions, a certain 'social capital' and regular access to FT markets. This impact is more visible in periods when international prices for exported products are low, or even very low. On balance, it is wise to say that Fair Trade protects producers and their families against extreme poverty rather than lifting them out of poverty.

5

Looking for the Global Impact of Fair Trade

> Over the last 20 years, Fairtrade has been extremely successful.
> Sales of Fairtrade-certified products have increased phenomenally.
> Marginalized farming communities throughout the world benefit from
> fairer trade conditions. And 2008 was no exception to this upward
> trend. (FLO, 2009b: 21)

Empirical arguments in favour of or against Fair Trade tend to focus on data relating to its local impact. However, this perspective is insufficient. A comprehensive evaluation should also take into account its global impact. In reality, this solidarity approach has an overall consistency that cannot be reduced to its local manifestations taken in isolation. The numerous cases of success here and there cannot be seen as a confirmation of the global impact of Fair Trade or of the possibility of extrapolating the benefits of this model. This is evidenced by the fact that the functions of the movement are not the same in the two cases. At the local level, Fair Trade seeks first and foremost to stabilise and increase the income of producers. At the global level, the movement seeks to provide an alternative to neoliberalism. On this point, one must distinguish between Fair Trade as global discourse and Fair Trade as global praxis.

As a discourse, it ought to be said that Fair Trade has had and continues to have a large media impact in the North, even if this goes along with a degree of confusion caused by the proliferation of 'ethical' labels. From our point of view, this is one of the aspects where its impact is clear and unambiguous (Hudson et al., 2013). This being said, we must also point out that this communication success was facilitated by the sensitisation effort led for several decades by alterglobalist (or Third Worldist) movements on the issue of unequal exchange and by the greater receptiveness of consumers vis-à-vis considerations pertaining to the origin and quality of consumption products.[1] On the other hand, there are reasons to believe that this media impact is far more limited in the South.

As a global praxis, Fair Trade takes on at least four functions. First, it seeks to transform trade practices and more or less to substitute itself for the conventional trade of products traditionally exported by the South. Second, as a self-proclaimed alternative to development assistance, Fair Trade plays a resource transfer function. Third, it has the function of global redistribution, as a movement that seeks to support the most marginalised or the poorest citizens of this planet. Finally, it seeks to become an alternative to conventional trade that pays attention to the specific case of countries that are dependent upon a limited number of export products. Indeed, the problems encountered by these countries often come up in arguments resorted to in order to justify the existence of Fair Trade.

If the assessment of the local impact of Fair Trade usually leads to mixed results that need to be qualified and interpreted with caution, things are different when it comes to its global impact. In the last analysis, as we are going to demonstrate, the alleged success of this new project lies more with the efficiency of the rhetoric of its protagonists than with a thorough demonstration of the benefits generated thus far.

A Non-Existent Global Economic Impact

A keen observer would not miss the subtleties of the modes of communication of Fair Trade protagonists. When it comes to showing that the movement is working, figures from consumer countries are presented, namely the growth in retail sales of FT products, or even opinion polls. However, when it comes to the impact in the South, pretty pictures and exotic testimonies are generally used. Such asymmetric communication does not facilitate the debate on the empirical impact of Fair Trade. Since the end purpose is to improve the living conditions of producers, the development of sales being but an intermediary objective, labelling initiatives should perhaps communicate more rigorously on this point.

Without a doubt, Fair Trade has proved a marketing success. In 2011 for instance, the global sales of FT products reached just under €5 billion. This spectacular development in the sales of FT products is a strong indicator of the vote of confidence from consumers and their willingness to join the daily struggle for fairer international trade in favour of poor producers. It also lends renewed legitimacy to labelling initiatives, which do not hesitate to communicate on these achievements in order to further sensitise consumers and donors.

To highlight the lack of relevance of Fair Trade, its detractors frequently show that it only represents a small proportion of international trade. However, such a comparison has two limitations. First of all, it is not because the market share of Fair Trade is low that its impact is necessarily low as well. Given that the poorest countries account for a very small part of international trade, small gains in market share can have significant effects. For example, according to Oxfam, if the share of Africa, South Asia, East Asia and Latin America in world exports increased by 1 per cent each, nearly 128 million people would be lifted out of poverty (Oxfam, 2002). Second, from a conceptual point of view, it is not really useful to compare the turnover of one sector (FT sales) with international trade (sum of exports and imports). A more relevant comparison would be between the export revenue from FT products and the global export revenue of developing countries (or, more specifically, between the export revenue from FT products and the value of exports from the South to the North). The problem is that information on the sums received in the South rarely receives as much visibility as figures on FT sales.

Low financial gains

Fair Trade makes two types of transfers to producers in the South: FT income (based on the FT minimum price) and the FT premium. The latter normally goes to producer organisations and should in principle be managed in a collegial and democratic way. The FT premium is meant to fund promising community projects: social infrastructure, development of production capacities, etc. FT income is also collected by producer organisations. Once certain costs have been deducted (namely administrative costs), they are then redistributed between the various members based on the contribution of each in terms of volumes sold. From an analytical point of view, such revenue has *a priori* more importance for three reasons at least. On the one hand, the amount of the FT premium depends on the volume of FT products sold. On the other, we must point out that part of this amount is destined for the annual renewal of FT certification. Thus, for organisations having made significant sales, the FT premium can be high. However, for those who have recorded low sales, the FT premium tends to be absorbed by the certification renewal.

Finally, every producer taken individually is concerned first and foremost with the income to be received.

According to a recent FLO publication entitled *The Benefits of Fairtrade 2008* (2010c), producer organisations and hired labour organisations in the South received close to €442 million on account of their FT product sales in 2008 (FT premium not included): €351 million went to the former and €91 million to the latter (namely plantation wage workers). I would like to make clear to readers that my arguments are based on the assumption that these amounts were indeed received in the South. Care must be taken, as some authors maintain that producers in the South do not always receive the FT premium.[2] Besides, it must be pointed out that these figures are based on reports following audits that took place between 2007 and 2009, and which covered 92 per cent of organisations having received FT certification (hired labour organisations in particular). As for producer organisations, the publication points out that the data is 'complete' (less than 1–2 per cent of observations are missing). From the point of view of statistical analysis, the data is therefore sufficiently representative.[3]

When we compare the €442 million to the total value of exports from developing countries ($6,200 billion in 2008) (see UNCTAD, 2010b: 2), it goes without saying that Fair Trade is a mouse hole in the big house of international trade. A way of illustrating this statement more vividly would be to divide the $6,200 billion by the number of hours in a year. One would then realise that the annual FT export revenue is more or less equivalent to the average value of an hour of exports from the South. Needless to say, at this rate Fair Trade actors will need a great deal of courage to significantly transform international trade.

However, it is not possible to assess the benefits of Fair Trade on the basis of this amount of €442 million. To put things in a simple way, the total net revenue received by FT producers and wage workers for their entire FT production is the sum of net revenue received on FT markets and non-FT markets (revenue of FT production sold on FT markets + revenue of FT production sold on non-FT markets). The €442 million only relates to the share of FT production sold on the FT market.[4] Due to the lack of detailed information on overall costs as well as gross revenue in non-FT markets, it was not possible to provide a total estimate of the total net revenue received in the South by FT producers and wage workers.

Yet, to realise how small the benefits from Fair Trade are, one can simply compare this export revenue to the number of workers in each case. We obtain an average of €415 for producers and €716 for wage workers.[5] For all workers combined, we obtain on average €454 in annual revenue. When taking into account workers and their families, there would be, according to FLO, close to 6 million people who rely on Fairtrade.[6] Based on this estimation, the annual average income per capita amounted to €74 in 2008. It goes without saying, obviously, that the purchasing power for this amount varies according to the context. Pronouncing any judgement on the benefits that one or the other might gain from such an amount becomes a delicate task. In spite of this obvious difficulty, there is no possible ambiguity on this subject. First of all, we should point out that these sums of €74 only represent 16 per cent of the average GDP per capita of LDCs.[7] Second, we ought to point out that the averages calculated so far are the gross income – in other words, costs (of production, transport, packaging, etc.) were not deducted (see Table 5.1).[8] Given how low they are, it is not random that these averages do not appear in the 'Facts and figures' section of the websites of some labelling initiatives.

Table 5.1   Gross FT revenue received in the South in 2008

	Gross annual FT revenue (in million €)	Number of workers (people) (in thousands)	Annual FT revenue/worker (person) in €
Producers	351	845	415
Wage workers	91	127	716
Total	442	972	454
Gains per person (workers and their families)	442	6,000	74
FT premium*	42.3	6,000	7

Note: *The FT premium is a gross transfer (the share relating to the renewal of FT certification is not counted).

Sources: For gross revenue, see FLO (2010c: 51–2); for the FT premium, see FLO (2010c: 36–7), for the number of producers and wage workers in 2008, see FLO (2010c: 7–8). These FT gains relate to the share of FT production sold according to FT trading conditions. The number of people (workers and their families) is based on FLO estimates provided in the 'Facts and figures' section of its website.

Such results will no doubt completely surprise many. However, those who tend to resist the ascendancy of marketing will be a little less surprised. In defence of Fair Trade, we must say that these results simply show that the net gains it generates are low. They certainly do not imply that non-FT producers or wage workers fare better. It may actually be that these are in a more distressing situation. If need be, this would better illustrate the important survival problems that workers in the South are generally facing.

As underscored by Chang (2008) with the examples of Nokia and Samsung, we cannot hope to lift people out of poverty by keeping them in low-productivity activities. They must challenge the market by doing things that are more difficult and yet more profitable. In spite of its many 'guarantees', Fair Trade is but the setting of a conservative minimum price and increased marketable agricultural production. The remainder (FT premium, sales, pre-financing, etc.) obeys the logic of the market. Some will no doubt be outraged by the communicational distortions of Fair Trade protagonists. But once again, one would be naive to hope that this economic model, as it has been designed, is able to generate considerable gains for millions of workers. Let us be clear: the much praised generosity of consumers of the North is not a credible basis for global social policy.

The value added remains in the North

In order to illustrate this last statement, the example of the United States is quite explicit. According to Transfair USA (2009), countries in the South received $34.7 million of 'additional income' – income above the market price + FT premium in 2008.[9] Let us now compare this amount with the turnover from FT sales in the United States, estimated at $1.1 billion in 2008.[10] It appears that the rate of transfer is at around $0.031. In other words, for each dollar paid by American 'consum'actors' to purchase an FT product, 3 cents of 'additional income' are transferred to the South. Given that this additional income was collected for the most part by coffee producers,[11] one can also assume that for each dollar spent in the purchase of this Fair Trade flagship product, 3 cents are transferred. With this rate of transfer and all other things being equal, FT sales would have to amount to $31.7 billion in order to generate additional income of $1 billion for the South. Do American consumers only transfer 3 cents for each FT product purchased or do they pay a higher surplus? I cannot answer this question. Nevertheless, it is likely that the surplus paid by consumers is higher. This would imply that the difference is captured by economic intermediaries.

Although low, this transfer is not a net figure. On the one hand, it includes the premium, which is a gross transfer (the amount used for the renewal of certification is not deducted). On the other, the 3 cents only apply to FT production sold at FT conditions. Given that FT producers seldom sell their whole FT production at FT conditions, it follows that in the best case scenario, the remainder is sold at market price. If the latter is lower than the FT minimum price, this can be considered a form of '*dumping*' in so far as this production is sold at a price that is unlikely to reflect its real cost (the cost of sustainable production). In such circumstances, producers of the South are the ones transferring a surplus to the North when the remainder is destined for exportation. Consumers in the North are unknowingly going to purchase goods that were produced according to FT standards, but obtained according to the usual market conditions. In other words, before talking about a net transfer from North to South, we need to have an idea of the net amount of the FT premium and of the possible foregone income incurred on the whole FT production.

The low level of the surplus transferred to the South is revealing of another major aspect, namely the fact that the value added of Fair Trade remains in the North. Indeed, most of its profits are hogged by economic actors based in the North (including labelling initiatives). The €442 million of FT export revenue only represented 15 per cent of the turnover from FT product sales in 2008 (16.7 per cent if we include the FT premium). *A priori*, compared with the percentages usually collected by producers in the agricultural value chains, this figure seems quite acceptable. Nevertheless, the fact is that Fair Trade did not enable producers in the South to access the most profitable markets along the agricultural value chains. And it has definitely not changed the margin-setting practices of distribution channels and large agrifood actors either. This is certainly unfortunate, as the goal of this movement is to maximise net financial gains for poor producers in the South by changing trade practices.

A relatively costly transfer system

In light of these elements, there is certainly cause for querying the efficiency of Fair Trade as a resource transfer mechanism. The main criticism from neoliberal critics is that it is no more effective than a unilateral transfer system without any charge, such as charity. We can no doubt witness a dialogue of the deaf on this point, as Fair Trade promotes first and foremost the logic of reciprocity. As a movement, it has always endorsed the slogan 'Trade not aid' and condemns charity on the basis that it undermines the dignity of producers in the South and leads to dependency. From the point of view of principles, the logic of reciprocity is certainly preferable to the logic of charity. However, if we look at it from the cold and cynical perspective of a cost–benefit analysis – a mode of evaluation that Fair Trade protagonists would not disavow, judging by the mode of calculation of the FT minimum price – the efficiency of Fairtrade as a resource transfer system seems rather low.

One of the functions of labelling initiatives and of FLO is to promote the sale of FT products via marketing and sensitisation campaigns. To this end, these organisations commit economic resources that can be analysed as costs from the point of view of the FT system as a whole. If we take into account the entire expenditure committed by all organisations for the promotion of Fair Trade, as well as the work done by hundreds of thousands of volunteers, the total cost induced is very likely higher than the net gains going to the South.

In 2008, the aggregated budget of five labelling initiatives (Germany, France, the United States, the United Kingdom and Switzerland) and FLO reached just under €31.2 million in 2008 (see Table 5.2). This

Table 5.2 Budget of selected labelling initiatives (in thousand €)

	2009		2008	
	Total budget (in thousand €)	Share of licensee fees in %	Total budget (in thousand €)	Share of licensee fees in %
Max Havelaar France	4,874	88.7	4,490	87.5
Transfair Germany	4,705	61.3	4,562	57.1
FLO*	6,356	n.a.	3,098	n.a.
Max Havelaar Switzerland **	3,564	99.5	3,585	95.6
Fairtrade Foundation United Kingdom**	10,990	75.5	9,097	85.6
Transfair USA **	6,840	68.8	6,335	62.1
Total	37,331	63.7	31,167	69.6
including fees (in thousand €)	23,762		21,685	

Notes: * Income from member dues was excluded. ** We used the average prevailing exchange rates; in 2009, income was measured in constant terms, that is using 2008 exchange rates.

Source: Germany: annual report 2009–10; United States: annual report and financial statements for the years ended 31 December 2008 and 2009; France: annual report 2009–10; FLO: annual report 2009–10; United Kingdom: annual report and financial statements for the year ended 31 December 2009; Switzerland: annual report 2009. All these documents are available for download on the websites of the relevant organisations.

amount is relatively close to the estimated amount of the FT premium (€42.3 million in 2008). Yet, it must be noted that the budgets of the 14 other labelling initiatives were not taken into account[12] and that the FT premium is a gross transfer. It is therefore very likely that the total budgets of labelling initiatives are at least higher than the net amount of the FT premium transferred to the South in 2008.

Besides, given that budgets of labelling initiatives are increasingly funded through licensing fees, it would appear that they have become a substitute for local intermediaries ('the coyotes') in the framework of the FT value chains. In comparison with exchanges involving local intermediaries, Fair Trade probably has a more positive outcome for producers in the South. This being said, the income received by labelling initiatives as entities in charge of marketing the Fairtrade label is relatively high compared with the FT net gains received by producers and wage workers in the South. For example, income generated through licensing fees in Germany, France, the United States, the United Kingdom and Switzerland reached €21.6 million in 2008. This represents on average 51 per cent of the gross amount of the FT premium. Quite obviously, the marginal utility of money is not the same in the North and in the South – a euro or dollar has greater value in the latter context. This in fact only confirms the observation that Fair Trade as a transfer system has low efficiency.

Besides, we can learn useful things about the case of Transfair USA[13] by cross-referencing data from one of its publications (Transfair USA, 2009) with the statement of income included in each of its annual reports (2001–9). Between 2001 and 2009, the Transfair USA budget increased 14-fold, rising from $686,000 to $10 million. Unsurprisingly, licensing fees have been the most dynamic line, increasing from $307,000 to $6.8 million (which amounts to a 22-fold increase). The least we can say is that Transfair USA (as much as most labelling initiatives) did not become impoverished through Fair Trade. It is also clear that average FT producers did not experience the same tremendous growth in net income. It may be true that income generated by licensing fees represents less than 1 per cent of the value of FT retail sales in the United States. Nevertheless, regarding the year 2009 for instance, these fees represented 20 per cent of additional income (premium not included) that the American FT market generated for producers and workers in the South (see Annexes: Tables A2 and A3).

In summary, the marketing success of Fair Trade should certainly not overshadow the fact that, after two decades of official existence, it remains an insignificant reality of international trade. Besides, the net gains received by producers in the South are low and probably offset by costs involved in the promotion of the movement. In the final analysis, one may be under the impression that the surplus paid by consumers is used to maintain a system which would otherwise find it difficult to remain at the forefront of the media scene.

Fair Trade Does Not Benefit the Poorest

As much as the gains obtained through Fair Trade are low, their distribution is just as unequal. This is not surprising. Given that the average net gains are low and that specific organisations seem to have greatly benefited from Fair Trade *a priori*, if we trust the statements made by labelling initiatives, it logically follows that the most significant benefits of this movement lean towards a minority.

Such inequality would be less problematic if it favoured producers from the poorest developing countries. The reality is that Fair Trade is mostly beneficial to the richest countries. To remove any suspense right away, we can say that only a minority of Latin American countries enjoy its financial rewards. On average, this region collects two-thirds of the FT premium (see FLO, 2010d, 2011). Likewise, Latin America and the Caribbean account for nearly 70 per cent of export revenue, followed by Africa (24 per cent) and the Asia-Oceania group (6 per cent) (FLO, 2011).

Fair Trade gains mostly benefit Latin America

To explain the unequal distribution of the gains of Fair Trade, we must examine the characteristics of both supply and demand in FT certification. Demand for FT certification emanates from producer or hired labour organisations, whereas the supply of FT certification depends upon FT labelling initiatives (namely FLO). An intermediary concept is that of effective certification demand – a concept referring to actually granted certification. Its analytical usefulness is based on two key considerations. On the one hand, producers may wish to seek FT certification without actually being able to obtain it (for example, there is no FT certification offer for the selected product, producers lack the means to pay for certification or they are unable to fulfil relevant conditions). In such circumstances, there is demand for FT certification, but it is not met. On the other hand, organisations having previously received FT certification may find themselves in a situation of non-renewal, or withdrawal of their certification (non-compliance with standards, problems linked to the payment for certification, unilateral withdrawal from the FT system, etc.). In other words, the notion of effective certification demand measures progress made in terms of certification by the FT/Max Havelaar movement for a little over two decades. Therefore, the statistics in this chapter sum up the performance of Fairtrade over close to 20 years.

The unequal distribution of the gains of Fair Trade derives in a large part from the characteristics of the certification offer. In actual fact, the FT certification system presents a two-fold bias against the poorest developing countries. First of all, there are considerations related to the costs of FT certification. These being the same everywhere, they are therefore in principle relatively more expensive for the most disadvantaged countries, all other things being equal.[14] Then, due to its sliding-scale price structure, FT certification is less costly for large producer organisations than for the smaller ones. Finally, the cost of compliance with FT standards (changes in agricultural and administrative practices that often lead to an increase in working hours) is higher for small organisations due to their lower productivity and to the lower economies of scale.

Besides, FT-certified articles tend to be based on products usually exported by Latin American countries. Coffee represents 36 per cent of the effective certification demand. Tea (9.3 per cent), fresh fruit and vegetables (9.1 per cent) and bananas (8 per cent) complete the list of top certified products in 2009.[15] Generally speaking, one out of two FT-certified products is either coffee, bananas or cocoa. In terms of export revenue, coffee is also the most sold FT product at 47 per cent, followed by bananas at 18.8 per cent.[16] In other words, coffee and bananas account for two-thirds of export revenue generated by Fair Trade. Yet, Latin America accounts for 263 out of the 317 FT coffee certifications granted in 2009 (or 83 per cent of FT coffee certifications) and 70 out of the 71 banana certifications (FLO, 2010e).

Let us pause and focus on the case of FT coffee. According to Transfair USA (2009), $196 million was distributed in the form of 'additional income' between 1998 and 2009. Of this amount, 96 per cent was received by coffee producers. Out of the $41 million of premium distributed, 81 per cent went to coffee producers. In volume terms, FT coffee imports by the United States for the period 2003–9 are distributed as follows: 80 per cent originate from Latin America against 14 per cent from Asia and 6 per cent from Africa. We must point out that the United States account for just over 20 per cent of FT product sales worldwide.

Fair Trade marginalises the poorest countries...

As we have just seen, Latin America enjoys a double benefit compared to Africa and Asia, namely that FT certification is less costly in its case and FT product markets are dominated by its main export products. The result of this bias in FT certification is that Latin America accounts for 56 per cent of effective certification demand against 29 per cent for Africa, 14 per cent for Asia and 1 per cent for Oceania. Though Latin American countries are no doubt among the most unequal in the world, they are certainly not among the poorest. A paradox not yet underscored is that Mexico is the first country where Fairtrade was tried out. Yet this OECD member state accounts for nearly a quarter of the GDP of Latin America and the Caribbean. Its GDP is actually higher than that of the whole of sub-Saharan Africa. Seen from this angle, it would seem that the FT system was biased right from the start.

We must therefore acknowledge the highly problematic nature of the categorical statement oft repeated by Fair Trade protagonists, according to which the movement is at the service of the poor. It no doubt helps poor and vulnerable producers, but it certainly is not at the service of the poorest. In fact, effective certification demand is positively correlated to the country income level. Countries ranked by the World Bank as *upper middle-income countries* account for 54 per cent of producer organisations having received FT certification against 21 per cent in the case of *low-income countries*. As for LDCs, they only account for 13.5 per cent of effective certification demand. In other words, whatever definition of poverty and economic vulnerability is used, the conclusion is the same: Fair Trade tends to exclude the poorest countries.

As a response on this point, labelling initiatives often resort to the rhetoric of marginalisation, which can be described as follows: 'We deal with the case of marginalised producers and wage workers.' There is evident bad faith in this argument, as the message conveyed to consumers and other marketing targets focuses on the case of the poorest. Beyond this, we must point out that such marginalisation rhetoric does not reflect reality. As shown in the previous chapter, Fairtrade selects the most capable producer organisations locally. This is actually its 'in-house policy', as it boosts the rapid growth of the movement.

This marginalisation rhetoric is mobilised by Alastair Smith (2008: 23–4) for example. In rich countries such as Mexico, he argues, there are huge social and economic inequalities as a result of which some populations find themselves in a situation of extreme poverty. This is undeniable, but not convincing in this case. First of all, this argument does not explain why within these inegalitarian countries, the least poor groups are generally selected by Fair Trade. Then, the criterion used to justify which nations deserve to enter the FT system is contradictory in this case. France, for example, is a very rich country. Yet it has many poor workers and farmers. So why not promote Fair Trade in France, as some have argued, or in the United States or the United Kingdom? Fair Trade protagonists will argue that these countries can tackle their own problems, as they have the means to do so. But this is also the case of Mexico and of the richest developing countries. Better still, differences in income between France and Mexico are much less pronounced than between Mexico and LDCs.[17] In fact, if we choose to favour Mexico over France based on the need criterion, the same logic should mean favouring the poorest countries at the expense of wealthier developing countries.

… as well as countries that are commodity-dependent

The fact that the richest developing countries capture most of the profits is certainly problematic from a distributive justice perspective. Beyond this, we must also underscore that Fair Trade gains are also channelled towards countries where the trade of primary products has the least macroeconomic impact.

The issue of unequal exchange has had the merit of showing that some countries are highly dependent upon the export of a limited number of primary products. The slightest price variation can have a significant impact on their economies. Within the FT system, dependent countries are under-represented whereas those countries with the most diversified exports are over-represented.

Let us take the case of coffee, a product with a major distributive advantage as it is mostly produced by small producer organisations. Ethiopia and Burundi are among the countries most dependent on coffee in the world. Coffee accounts for 34 per cent and 26 per cent of their export revenue respectively. For both these countries, only three FT coffee certifications were issued in 2009, mostly for Ethiopia; Burundi was not yet covered by the FT system. In contrast, Mexico and Peru received 42 and 57 FT certifications respectively, which represents nearly 31 per cent of the effective certification demand for FT coffee. Yet these two economies are relatively diversified and, at any rate, coffee exports account for less than 2 per cent of their export revenue. In Latin America, Honduras and Nicaragua are two countries relying greatly on coffee. In relative terms, their dependency on coffee is at least ten times higher than that of Mexico and Peru. But their share of the effective FT coffee certification demand is lower.[18]

FT bananas, cocoa and cotton follow a similar narrative. The countries most dependent on these products are under-represented in the FT system. Among flagship products, only FT tea seems to be an exception. Yet, one of its specificities (as for bananas, flowers and plants, fruit and vegetables) is that it is produced primarily by male and female wage workers in plantations (see Table 5.3).

How can the exclusion of poor countries be explained?

This exclusion of LDCs and other vulnerable developing countries is not the result of a deliberate choice by FT labelling initiatives. Indeed, the movement especially seeks to help those that already are on its 'path', in other words, producer organisations showing a development potential and organisational predispositions. We already had the opportunity to discuss this microeconomic dimension in the previous chapter. Beyond this elitist approach, two additional considerations of a macroeconomic nature must be taken into account.

To begin with, the path taken by Fair Trade is much too narrow for poor countries to tread on. Let me explain. Fair Trade chose to specialise in the trade of agricultural products. This choice of specialisation is based on a specific vision of unequal exchange inspired from the Latin American context.

It is true that LDCs are generally countries where the labour force is primarily employed in agriculture. The problem is, however, that LDCs are often dependent to a greater extent on the export of non-agricultural primary products. UNCTAD only ranks 11 out of a total of 49 countries as exporters of agricultural products (over 50 per cent of export revenue). To make matters more complex, most LDCs are net importers of food products. With the exception of three countries, all LDCs are part of the

Table 5.3 Number of FT certifications according to the degree of commodity dependency

	Number of certifications (2009)	% of total export revenue
Coffee (317 FT certifications)		
Ethiopia	3	34.1
Burundi	0	26.2
Uganda	3	21.9
Honduras	24	20.5
Nicaragua	20	18.5
Rwanda	6	15.1
Guatemala	18	8.5
Colombia	38	5.9
Peru	52	1.8
Bolivia	22	<1.2
Mexico	47	<2.3
Banana (71 FT certifications)		
Dominica	0	20.0
Costa Rica	2	7.3
Saint-Vincent and the Grenadines	1	15.9*
Saint Lucia	0	13.3*
Ecuador	7	8.8***
Panama	0	8.6***
Dominican Republic	23	<1.6
Colombia	26	1.7
Peru	8	<1.8
Tea (82 FT certifications)		
Rwanda	2	26.8
Kenya	17	18.0
Sri Lanka	12	14.3
Malawi	5	5.3
Burundi	0	4.5
Uganda	4	3.1
Tanzania	7	1.4
India	18	<1.6
Cotton (37 FT certifications)		
Benin	0	48.8
Burkina Faso	2	36.1
Mali	4	12.0
Togo	0	9.1
Tanzania	0	4.8
Cameroon	1	4.3
India	16	<1.6
Senegal	10	<2.0
Chad	0	n.a.
Cocoa (39 FT certifications)		
São Tome and Principe	0	49.3
Ghana	1	28.4
Côte d'Ivoire	7	26.8
Cameroon	1	9.5
Grenada	0	5.0
Papua New Guinea	0	4.1
Ecuador	3	1.5
Nicaragua	4	<2.6
Peru	9	<1.8
Dominican Republic	4	<1.6

Notes: * 24.5% in 2007; ** 25.3% in 2007; *** 14.5% in 2009; **** 10% in 2007.

Source: FLO (2010e), *UNCTAD Handbook of Statistics, 2009* (UNCTAD, 2010b: ch. 3.2.D, 163–80) and UN Comtrade (2010). For each product, we selected the most dependent countries and those with the higher number of certifications. The country profiles from the *UNCTAD Handbook of Statistics, 2009* and those from UN Comtrade (2010) only include the first ten export products. When the given product is not included in this list (as is the case for coffee in Mexico and Bolivia), we estimated its share of the export revenue by using that of the tenth exported product as a reference. In the case of bananas especially, the export revenue data is taken from the 2009 country profiles developed by UN Comtrade. With the exception of bananas and Tanzania (as far as tea is concerned), all other export-related data comes from UNCTAD. In the case of cotton, economies in transition were excluded.

category defined by the FAO as 'Low-Income Food-Deficit Countries' (see Table 5.4).

Table 5.4 Distribution of LDCs according to their trade structure

Category (number)	Countries
Exporters of agricultural products (11)	Afghanistan, Benin, Burkina Faso, Guinea-Bissau, Solomon Islands, Kiribati, Liberia, Malawi, Uganda, Somalia, Tuvalu
Exporters of manufactured products (6)	Bangladesh, Bhutan, Cambodia, Haiti, Lesotho, Nepal
Exporters of minerals (10)	Burundi, Guinea, Mali, Mauritania, Mozambique, Niger, Central African Republic, Democratic Republic of Congo, Sierra Leone, Zambia
Mixed exporters (5)	Madagascar, Myanmar, Lao People's Democratic Republic, Senegal, Togo
Petroleum and fuel exporters (6)	Angola, Chad, Equatorial Guinea, Sudan, Timor-Leste, Yemen
Exporters of services (11)	Comoros, Djibouti, Eritrea, Ethiopia, Gambia, Maldives, Rwanda, Samoa, Sao Tomé and Principe, United Republic of Tanzania, Vanuatu

Source: UNCTAD (2010a). Malawi exited the LDC group in 2011 and Samoa will follow suit in 2014; the Maldives, Samoa and Myanmar were the only LDCs not included in the FAO's Low-income Food-deficit Countries (FAO, 2010).

Therefore, Fair Trade tends to mostly benefit Latin American countries because this region is a net exporter of agricultural products (see Annexes: Table A4). A country like Argentina, for instance, draws half of its export revenue from agricultural products (see WTO, 2009: 50). To put things differently, agriculture in Latin America is mostly focused on exports, whereas for African and Asian LDCs, agriculture serves a subsistence purpose.

This configuration actually explains why some economists are rather cautious about the impact of the liberalisation of agricultural product markets in the North. Subsidies granted to rice, dairy products, etc. no doubt harm developing countries that export the same products. However, for those importing such products, removing these distortions can have tragic economic consequences (Bureau et al., 2006; Stiglitz and Charlton, 2005: 122). In a report that followed an unprecedented rise in the price of agricultural products, the FAO said: 'In 2007, the total cost of importing food products for developing countries was already higher by 33 per cent in comparison to 2006, and the annual bills for the food product imports of low-income food-deficit countries had doubled from their level in 2000' (FAO, 2009: 29).[19] Unfortunately, proponents of absolute free trade do not pay much attention to this type of consideration.

In a sense, the 'mistake' made by founders of Fairtrade and of the movement that they helped to establish was to believe that what applied to the Latin American context could also work in other developing regions. If Fair Trade had been born in the African context, it would probably have had a greater focus on mining or petroleum products. Likewise, if it had been inspired in Asia, it would probably have been more specialised in the trade of textile products and clothing.

Beyond its narrowness, the path trodden by Fair Trade follows contours drawn by the market. Why would an American importer of FT products seek coffee with a specific quality far into the depths of Ethiopia while it can be obtained in Mexico at a lesser cost? In comparison to Ethiopia, Mexico presents significant competitive advantages: it belongs to NAFTA – the North American Free Trade Agreement (hence customs procedures are more flexible and less costly) – and it is geographically close to the United States, its agricultural producers are on average more productive, etc. In such circumstances, without actual willingness to initiate trade relations of a progressive nature and to radically transform their geographical structure, there is *a priori* no reason at all why such an importer would look for more expensive supplies in the Horn of Africa.

In fact, in the area of bilateral trade, empirical research has isolated two crucial determinants: the geographical distance between countries and their economic size. It seems in reality that international trade is all about 'clubs': all other things being equal, the rich trade more with other rich than with the poor. This is justified by their different levels of development.[20]

Evidence of this is that, outside of all plutocratic logic, it is difficult to identify a consistent *pattern* to the expansion of FT certification in some areas of the globe. In sub-Saharan Africa, the country with the richest economy (in GDP terms), South Africa, tops FT certification demand with 54 out of a total of 260 in 2009. Its two major FT products are 'fresh fruit and vegetables' and 'wine grapes', products that are not part of the country's top ten exports. In Asia, India accounted for 56 of the 124 FT certifications that were granted in 2009. Its two major FT products are cotton and tea. These are not part of its ten major exports either.[21] Judging from the products traditionally exported by these countries, FT products listed here appear as exotic oddities, finding themselves here randomly because the statistics of the movement must be pushed up (including its income). However, to this end, there is no more effective strategy than to take advantage of the scale effect associated with economic size.

All other things being equal, it is probably normal that the number of certifications should be higher for countries with a large market and a higher than average purchasing power. This plutocratic bias leads to a major contradiction, however: the genuine 'targets' of Fair Trade tend to be sidestepped in favour of exotic clients entering the FT system simply because they are fortunate to live in a country with a larger than average market. Thus, dependent countries among the poorest on the planet tend to be excluded in favour of others such as India, Mexico and South Africa that have less of a need for Fair Trade *a priori*.

Another way of illustrating this plutocratic bias is to look at the regional distribution of hired labour organisations (25 per cent of the total of organisations having received FT certification in 2009). Let us start by pointing out that Africa is on average the region that most employs workers in agriculture and which has one of the lowest shares of wage employment in the world.[22] The paradox is that it is under-represented among FT producer organisations whereas it is over-represented among FT hired labour organisations (namely those in plantations). Indeed, if we were to focus on this latter group only, Africa would have accounted for just over one out of two FT certifications in 2009. In other words, Africa is doing better than Latin America on this point! How can we explain this paradox? Our hypothesis is that the FT movement is having difficulties settling outside Latin America because it focuses for the most part on coffee and bananas. Yet it ought to be present everywhere. The problem is that small producers in LDCs are not sufficiently structured and, more importantly, they are very poor. As a result, in this type of context, the private economic groups that have purchasing power and know how to make the most of the Fair Trade tool are the ones joining the movement. Indeed, in contexts where poverty is high, Fair Trade often leads to difficult choices (see Box 5.1).

Beyond these demand-side considerations (purchasing power, economic size, etc.), we must point out that the plutocratic logic is also enhanced by supply effects. As a general rule, the level of economic development is positively correlated with the World Bank's *Logistics Performance Index*, which measures the ease of conducting trade. In sub-Saharan Africa, South Africa has the highest score in this respect. This is also the case for India in South Asia (World Bank, 2010b).

> **Box 5.1**   The dilemma of a Rwandan cooperative:
> excluding the poorest of the poor or leaving the FT system
>
> In order to provide a more sociological illustration of the plutocratic bias of
> Fair Trade, we can refer to a very interesting article by Jonathan Penson (2007),
> a teacher/education specialist who spent time with producers in Uganda and
> Rwanda. The case described here is that of a cooperative of FT coffee producers
> based in Rwanda. He narrates that some producers were forced to sell their
> coffee in advance, due to short-term cash flow problems. They were unable to
> wait until the time of the harvest to be paid by the cooperative. They had no
> access to credit and had no means to repay loans and attached interest. Other
> producers were too poor to join the cooperative. Either they were unable to
> pay the cooperative membership costs, or they did not have access to enough
> land to produce the minimum coffee amounts required to join the cooperative.
> Faced with these desperate cases, the policy of the cooperative was to allow
> the poorest to sell their coffee at FT conditions. This infringed FT standards.
> Unsurprisingly, the cooperative received an injunction to comply with FT
> standards under penalty of seeing its FT certification withdrawn. According
> to an official quoted by Penson, the Western demands for universality and
> transparency as embedded in the Fair Trade concept are not culturally
> compatible with African trade systems, which take circumstances into account
> as well as the nature of social relations. According to Penson, Fair Trade is
> increasingly perceived as an unsatisfactory response by Africans who tend to
> seek alternative solutions. He gives the example of a Ugandan private company
> that pays a 30 per cent bonus above market price for coffee and also shares
> 50 per cent of its profits with the 10,000 producers it works with. Its profits
> are allocated to training and the funding of social projects (schools, housing,
> etc.). This enterprise receives support from an NGO funded by USAID (United
> States Agency for International Development) and seeks to create and 'retain'
> value added in Uganda. While we could still question the generalisable or
> sustainable nature of such an initiative, it is nevertheless the case that it is a
> discreet and effective form of solidarity economy.

In a nutshell, although low, the gains of Fair Trade for the most part go to Latin American countries. In its global operations, Fair Trade does not partake in a logic of international redistribution in favour of the poorest countries, or even of dependent countries. In reality, this movement seems to follow a plutocratic logic, in other words, one that serves the government of the rich.

Quite obviously, notions of 'rich' and 'poor' are used here in a relative sense. On a global level, the rich are the labelling initiatives that created a rent for themselves thanks in part to the FT licensing fees, and which have certainly not become impoverished through Fair Trade. The same can also be argued with regard to FT licence holders and other distribution networks. On a regional level, the rich are the producer organisations of specific Latin American countries such as Mexico. On the national and local levels, they refer to the groups that can comply with market criteria (paying for certification, producing the required amounts, etc.). As we can see, the pro-market logic of Fair Trade leads to the status quo (the poor remain poor), to a degree of polarisation (the rich become richer at the expense of the poor) and to ignoring the needs of the poor[23] (those most reliant on primary products are marginalised). What is striking is that the protagonists and supporters of Fair Trade still have not realised this. The funniest part is that these detractors of free trade are usually unaware that each cup of Max Havelaar coffee that is drunk in the world is a tribute paid to the glory of 'Mr Market'.

Fair Trade: an Alternative to Neoliberalism?

At this juncture, a crucial question must be asked. Is Fair Trade an alternative to neoliberal globalisation? According to its co-founders, the Max Havelaar label was created in order to become 'a genuine alternative to the established order of international trade and development aid, as a model of globalisation from the bottom' (Roozen and van der Hoff, 2002: 238). If we set rhetoric aside and look closely at how Fair Trade has operated until now, it is difficult to rationally subscribe to this type of statement.

The success of Fair Trade is due to its compatibility with neoliberalism

While it is inaccurate to describe the Fairtrade movement as neoliberal, there is no doubt on the other hand that it owes its success to its compatibility with neoliberalism; on this, we are in complete agreement with Fridell (2007). To be more precise, we can even say that Fairtrade is an alternative to neoliberalism only from the point of view of its intentions and rhetoric, both of which are rather progressivist. Beyond these two aspects, this movement fundamentally follows a neoliberal logic.

From the point of view of its genesis, one could say that Fairtrade was born on a field already owned by neoliberalism. Its birth followed the neoliberal policies implemented all over the world since the 1980s, which resulted in the dismantling of the various national and international mechanisms initially set up to protect countries of the South from random market occurrences. As an approach, Fairtrade is therefore difficult to conceive of in a context where the trade of primary products is strongly regulated at the national and international levels. In this sense, the political space that it occupies presupposes a level of deregulation of the mechanisms that drive the world economy, or at least an institutional and legal void. Retrospectively, Fair Trade probably did not randomly focus on handicrafts at its beginning.

According to Karl Polanyi, the rise of capitalist laissez-faire was historically accompanied by counter-tendencies that sought to protect society from the destructive excesses of market logic (Polanyi, 2001 [1944]). On this basis, some authors asked whether the emergence of Fair Trade was not part of the dynamic of a Polanyian 'double movement' (Bacon, 2010; Guthman, 2007). The following elements do not seem to confirm such an assumption.

From a practical point of view, the success of FT sales results mostly from their integration into traditional distribution channels and their recuperation by agrifood multinationals. Without the help of the very market actors that it claims to be fighting, this movement would no doubt have stirred up less controversy. After all, if Fairtrade was able to get the better of historical/alternative Fair Trade, it is because it managed to overcome the ideological barrier and show more reformist pragmatism.

From a theoretical standpoint, the mode of calculation of the FT minimum price and the modalities for FT market operations are perfectly in line with the neoclassical scheme of free trade: labour power is but another input, tagged with a price that can be determined 'objectively' on the local rural market; producers are considered as small enterprises – this tends to hide their consumption needs; prices above the minimum price depend upon the outcome of negotiations between buyers and sellers; as for access to FT markets, it is subject to convoluted considerations about efficiency; traders are not required to commit to particular amounts and they can choose between FT and non-FT markets.

From the standpoint of the structures and rules of international trade, Fair Trade daily operations rely on the very optimistic assumption that international trade can be a development tool in the South, in spite of the asymmetric rules that characterise it. As a result, Fair Trade trades with the richest developing countries that have a tradition of export and are the least dependent upon the export of primary products. The net gains it helps to generate are low, as it relies on a logic of comparative advantage, focusing on activities that have low productivity and are less likely to provide technological and industrial spillovers. Unsurprisingly, the most sold FT goods are those that are not produced in the North and are the least taxed in the world (namely, coffee). In other words, Fair Trade does not change the geography of trade flows; it tends to exacerbate the unequal distribution of trade benefits, as it tends to exclude poor countries and poor local producers; it hides the issue of dependency on primary products; it does not significantly strengthen the position of producers along value chains; and, finally, it relies on the trade of products that suffer the least from barriers in the framework of the conventional international trading system.

One must therefore acknowledge that Fair Trade has positioned itself in opportunistic fashion as an alternative to neoliberalism in order to gain in stature. Rhetoric can often be virulent vis-à-vis the neoliberal paradigm. In reality, there is an elective affinity between this movement and the enemy it claims to be fighting. What must be understood clearly is that Fair Trade enjoys a dialectical relationship with the market system as organised by neoliberalism. On the one hand, it needs the neoliberal market system to attract the economic resources necessary to occupy a comfortable position in the concert of alterglobalist voices. On the other, to justify its successes, it needs its destructive support. Indeed, without the yardstick provided by neoliberalism, Fair Trade would have had difficulties pleading its cause publicly.

In the case of coffee, at a time when the terms of the International Agreement on Coffee were still in force (1962–89), producing countries received better prices and a higher share of the value added generated by retail sales in the North. According to Daviron and Ponte (2005: 120), the international coffee price between 1950 and the end of the 1990s was on average more or less twice as high as the price that would have prevailed on less regulated markets. It would also seem that producing countries earned on average close to 20 per cent of the income generated by the coffee value chain in the 1970s–1980s, against 13 per cent for the period 1980–95. In consumer countries, this figure went from 55 per cent to 78 per cent between these two dates and could even have increased in the recent period (Daviron and Ponte, 2005: ch. 6).

These observations therefore point to the paradox that, at a time when the Keynesian paradigm was dominant, the market system had 'fairer' effects for producers in the South than under the auspices of Fair Trade. A way of resolving this contradiction is to recognise that the definition of what is 'fair' and what is not is a matter of power relations. Fair Trade defined this notion in reference to the maximum limit of generosity allowed by the market, at a time when major economic actors became as powerful, if not more so than states. However, a definition of fairness linked to a sustainable and balanced partnership would most likely be based on the unconstrained and free expression of producers in the South.

The reality is that Fair Trade, from a practical viewpoint, is simply not a match for neoliberalism. What positive impact this movement has had in a little over 20 years of official existence does not even remotely compare with the economic, social and environmental disasters caused by the implementation of the tenets of neoliberalism over more than three decades.

A model of global redistribution that taxes labour in favour of capital

As it is practised, Fair Trade still leaves a lot to be desired as a redistribution mechanism. In a globalised world, a consistent redistribution principle could be structured as follows. First, the transfer should be made by a rich country in favour of a poor country. Second, the transfer should emanate from a rich citizen and reach a poor citizen. Third, inequalities should decrease, both in the donating country and in the receiving country.[24] In the case of Fair Trade, the main problem is the following: can we really talk about a net transfer from the North to the South?

As we have seen, the calculation of the cost of sustainable production is based on the market value of the labour force and not on an amount that would enable workers in the South to pull out of poverty in a lasting manner. In this sense, Fair Trade perpetuates the logic of labour force exploitation in the sphere of production. In fact, the 'sustainable' in the 'cost of sustainable production' refers to the fact that the FT minimum price, as it is calculated, ensures access to more sustainable markets and makes the movement more prosperous. It certainly does not imply that producers and their families can continue to make a decent and sustainable living on the basis of the FT minimum price. In other words, even under the auspices of Fair Trade, producers and wage workers in the South continue to be exploited and to transfer a surplus to the North, but certainly to a lesser degree and in a less apparent fashion than in the usual situations where this movement is not present.

Beyond this, even if we borrow the reasoning of Fair Trade protagonists, it is not any easier to talk about a net transfer from North to South due to the lack of information on the net amount of the FT premium and the foregone income possibly incurred over the FT production as a whole. At any rate, the fact remains that the net transfer rate from consumers to the South is very low. It would probably be null or even negative if we factored in the *dumping* scenario mentioned earlier, in which case the two initial criteria would probably not be filled. This comment is valid for the third criterion as well.

The benefits derived from an involvement in the FT system can certainly contribute to a marginal reduction of social and economic inequalities in the South between rural producers and urban workers. Yet, the very fact that it is up to consumers in the North – and not economic intermediaries – to pay more in order to sustain producers in the South may seem odd as a redistribution approach.[25] Besides, given that this surplus is certainly hogged by economic intermediaries, it goes without saying that Fair Trade was not created to reduce social and economic inequalities in the North. In the last analysis, the workers in the North and in the South end up paying the price for Fair Trade's quest, whereas conversely, the enterprises are the ones collecting most of the profit; in many respects therefore, and as Fair Trade protagonists will no doubt acknowledge, this approach is favoured by neoliberalism.[26]

An approach that is too politically correct

Finally, we must acknowledge that Fair Trade owes part of its success to the fact that as a development approach, it is one that is easier to sell on the political and media levels than some of the other existing alternatives. To illustrate this point, let us look at three important alternatives that were already offered in the framework of the fight against global poverty.

From a historical point of view, international labour movements from the South to the North were a factor in economic catching-up for specific nations that were previously at a disadvantage. In fact, one of the specificities of globalisation in its current form is that, in opposition to the previous 'wave', international labour movements from the South to the North are now rather weak, especially for low-skilled or unskilled workers.[27] Whatever the case might be, financial transfers made by migrants – from the South and settled in the North – to their countries of origin are higher than Official Development Assistance (nearly double in 2007; see Ratha and Mohapatra, 2007). While local economic impacts might be significant, most analyses agree that these could be further increased by the introduction of more suitable public policies (UNDP,

2009; United Nations, 2006). Along the same lines, according to some authors, a small increase in South–North labour movements would generate more advantages for developing countries than all the gains hoped for from market liberalisation processes in the North, as currently negotiated at the WTO.[28] So much so that many economists are convinced that migration is the best tool against global poverty (Milanovic, 2010; Pritchett, 2006).

Second initiative: reducing the trade barriers maintained by developed countries vis-à-vis exports from developing countries. Let us simply look at the case of LDCs. They account for less than 1 per cent of the total imports from rich countries, not including oil. A broader access to OECD markets could thus be very beneficial for their economies without costing much for the latter (Elliott, 2010).

Third initiative: in order to reach Millennium Development Goals (see Box 5.2), rich countries pledged to allocate 0.7 per cent of their Gross National Income to Official Development Assistance at the G8 Summit in Gleneagles and at the 2005 UN Global Summit. In spite of several reminders and attempts at pressure from the international community, most rich countries are struggling to keep these commitments.[29]

Each of these propositions presents a potential for generating significant benefits for the populations of developing countries. Not

---

Box 5.2 Millennium Development Goal 8:
A global partnership for development

In 2000, heads of states the world over defined and adopted eight key goals of economic policy that must be met by 2015. Among these Millennium Development Goals, one especially deserves a special mention here. It is the MDG on 'establishing a partnership for development'. It includes targets and related follow-up indicators.

- Address the special needs of the LDCs, landlocked countries and Small Island developing states.
- Develop further an open, rule-based, predictable, non-discriminating trading and financial system.
- Deal comprehensively with developing countries' debt.
- In cooperation with pharmaceutical companies, provide access to affordable essential drugs in developing countries.
- In cooperation with the private sector, make available the benefits of new technologies, especially information and communication.

Source: United Nations (2010).

only are they more effective in terms of global poverty reduction, but also easier to implement from a practical point of view, provided that an agreement exists. The problem is that they require very stringent international solidarity mechanisms that are incompatible with the fear of otherness cultivated by the neoliberal logic of extreme international competition. The hypocrisy of rich countries in their relations with developing countries lies to some extent in the fact that they privilege measures whose effectiveness is more symbolic than actual. The irony is that, at a time when Fair Trade supporters and protagonists drown their postmodernist anguish in the ecstatic whirl of FT product consumption, their governments continue to ask developing countries to further open up their economies while they lock themselves up in unprecedented protectionism. However, by promoting tailored forms of international solidarity that are not based on any commitment towards cultural openness, this approach runs the risk of becoming a new opium for those who want to fight against global poverty. Instead of reducing the gap between producers in the South and consumers in the North, Fair Trade may even further enhance commodity fetishism.

In summary, if Fair Trade is increasingly perceived, rightly or wrongly, as a solution to global poverty, it is because its protagonists chose the easiest path when raising the issue of a North–South partnership. This is a model so conciliatory in appearance that everyone stands to gain from it. It promises producers that the market system will not harm them as much as in the past. It aroused the pride of Northern consumers by elevating them to the status of politically committed global citizens whose purchasing power can transform millions of lives. It reassures 'Big Capital' that its stakes will not be harmed and that they can work together in a natural harmony of interests. As for institutions and governments in the North that do not have the time or willingness to help the poor, they find a new way out. Finally, regarding governments of the South, described as powerless, corrupt, inefficient and apathetic, Fair Trade offers to take on the issue of poverty under their nose. But it is precisely because this Fair Trade is 'fair' to everyone that it is problematic.

Conclusion

A good cause is often injured more by ill-timed efforts of its friends than by the arguments of its enemies. (Thomas Jefferson, letter to James Heaton, 20 May 1826)

This book was not written for the purpose of casting an anathema on Fair Trade. Quite to the contrary, I acknowledge that it is a praiseworthy approach, which proposes solutions to the adversities of globalisation today. It is precisely on account of this inherent value that light must be shed on the declared objectives of this movement and on its theoretical potential as a self-proclaimed alternative to neoliberalism. Besides, as someone from a country ranked amongst the least developed, I could not help but examine to what extent Fair Trade provides a satisfactory response to the difficulties encountered in such a context and takes its specificities into account. My objective is to demonstrate that while borne on good intentions, this movement is plagued by contradictions whose scope is not yet fully grasped by its protagonists. This being said, it should not be excluded that the ideas presented in this book are partly valid for private labelling initiatives as a whole, as well as for some strategies seeking to ensure that the free market also serves the poor, as the same structural logic produces the same effects. Likewise, although neoliberal critics will likely see it as a source of satisfaction, this book is in fact a Pyrrhic victory for this current. Indeed, its conclusions and recommendations radically depart from those shared by both supporters of Fair Trade and its critics from the neoliberal bent.

International trade did not prove to be the economic catch-up tool hoped for, due among other reasons to rich countries manipulating the rules that structure it. It has generated considerable profit for some developing countries. But for most others, it has rather proved to be a handicap. It is in this context that Fair Trade appeared in its labelled version at the end of the 1980s, aiming to initiate an 'ethical' consumption movement promoting trade practices that enable producers of the South to increase their income, and thus improve their living conditions and protect their environment.

At the outset however, the movement was faced with a dilemma: a choice had to be made between preserving the purity of the doctrinal principles and the need to extend market access for Fair Trade products. By choosing to remain faithful to their convictions, the pioneers of this solidarity approach implicitly condemned the trade of 'Fair' products to remain merely a symbolic initiative. With the advent of Fairtrade, these products become standardised and more broadly accessible to consumers on the strength of the pact sealed with the great enemies of yesteryear: the distribution channels and the multinational agribusinesses. This helped the movement to gain an audience and become well known. The price for this success is that Fairtrade lost some of its doctrinal consistency. It is neither neoliberal, nor really anti-neoliberal.[1] It is a new alterglobalist movement that thrives on rather curious ethical standards. These standards are such that some economic actors with a controversial ethical history – under the pretext of contributing to development in the South – can engage in Fair Trade for a minute part of their purchases and pursue their reprehensible practices of yesteryear for the rest. This turnaround of principle is actually what distinguishes these new proponents of Fair Trade from protagonists of historic Fair Trade who have always promoted an alternative trade approach distinct from the distribution channels and the large agrifood businesses.

But the contradictions go beyond the principles. They apply both to the economic model from which the movement draws its inspiration and to its outcomes. Fairtrade promised development on the economic, social and environmental levels. In the end, the net financial gains that reach producers in the South are meagre. Just like Don Quixote, Fairtrade had also promised to help the poor, the vulnerable and the needy. But in the end, the complete opposite happened. Generally speaking, Fairtrade trades with the richest countries and those that are the least dependent on the export of basic commodities. Locally, it tends to select the most dynamic groups that show some potential. Its local impact is most obvious in contexts where market prices are low and large quantities of FT products are sold. On the whole, it is more accurate to say that Fairtrade protects producers and their families from extreme poverty rather than taking them out of poverty.

Fairtrade claims to be an alternative to development aid in its various forms. Yet, the surplus paid by consumers and which is supposed to go to the South actually stays in the North, absorbed in all likelihood by economic intermediaries (distribution channels, major agrifood actors and labelling initiatives). At the current rate of development and given the rate of transfer now observed, FT sales for an amount of $31.7 billion would be necessary, if all things remained equal, to generate an additional $1 billion revenue for the South. This means that in spite of its imperfections, development assistance still has a major role to play.

These contradictory results may come as an awful and unimaginable revelation for supporters of Fairtrade, especially those on the ground. They will no doubt feel 'betrayed' by the free market whose natural tendencies quickly came bursting in. Fairtrade wanted to keep the market in check. In the end, it is the latter that leads it by the nose. Its protagonists and supporters will nevertheless learn that the free market rationale seldom benefits the poor, in spite of any willingness to redeem itself.

The phrase 'coffee paradox' was coined to reflect the coexistence of the coffee industry boom in the North and the social and economic crisis experienced by coffee producers in the South. It may perhaps also be time to speak about the 'Fair Trade paradox': media and marketing success in the North, alongside an insignificant or non-existent impact in the South.

However, this cannot entirely be put down to the 'betrayal' of the market. There is also the fact that the Fairtrade business model includes many weaknesses. It should be acknowledged that this movement focused on the marketing aspect and moral philosophy, rather than on a thorough and empirically informed economic analysis. The inability of Fairtrade to provide a solution to poverty derives, among other things, from its inconsistent price theory and the fact that it overlooks the counter-productive approach of the increased commodification of labour power. In actual fact, its objective is first and foremost to protect itself against the uncertainties of the market. Which is not the same as saying that it is attempting to eradicate poverty, as this would require tackling inequalities in all its forms (class, gender, ethnic, geographical) and possibly a resort to non-economic instruments (legislation for instance).

Another problem in the FT business model lies with its institutional assumptions. Its protagonists tend to assume that their approach is valid and relevant in all poor regions of the world. In doing this, they were led by a universalist approach to not take into account the specificities of LDCs and to unwittingly exclude them from the movement. The problem is that African and Asian LDCs usually export non-agricultural products: oil and mining products for the former, textiles and clothing for the latter. Fairtrade is in actual fact an issue relevant to Latin America and to coffee and banana producers. Beyond the context of economies based on export agriculture, it is difficult to identify any sense of consistency to the certification approach of this movement other than the plutocratic rationale, whose effect is to inflate statistics, including its own gains.

In the last analysis, the problem with Fairtrade is that it made too many promises, provided too many 'guarantees', showed too much chivalry, is too rhetorical ... in a word, it is too Quixotic. Yet, Fairtrade runs the risk of being perceived, rightly or wrongly, as the alternative for developing countries. Respected institutions and personalities are beginning to give this movement much credit, while its apparent success is based more on rhetorical prowess than on a convincing demonstration of its achievements. As a general rule, those who genuinely want to help, such as the protagonists of the Fairtrade movement, are an important part of the problem for which solutions are sought. Indeed in the area of development, 'self-righteousness is often more stubborn than self-interest' (Chang, 2008: 17).

This is evidenced by the fact that, in spite of their ever greater ambitions, Fairtrade protagonists still have not come to realise the extent to which recent developments have rendered their movement anachronistic. First, agricultural products have been experiencing a trending decline for many decades now. They now account for only 9 per cent of the international merchandise trade, while processed agricultural products represent two-thirds of exchanged goods. In the case of LDCs, however, they merely accounted for 0.3 per cent of this latter market in the period 1991–2000 (FAO, 2004: 26). By focusing on primary agricultural products, Fairtrade is pulling developing countries back. Besides, it does not allow them to envisage local industrial processing, which creates more value added and is more profitable in the long term.

Second, South–South trade has now become more significant than North–South trade.[2] So nothing justifies the delineation of Fair Trade exclusively along North–South lines. In the framework of trade relations, exploitation is not a matter of level of development. It is based on the logic of capital accumulation. It would be really unfortunate to assume that major economic actors in emerging countries have more 'ethical' practices towards the poorest countries than multinationals based in the North.

A third element is that the 'Fair Trade Company' has unknowingly become the target of a takeover bid. The future of 'ethical' trade, whether 'Fair', 'sustainable' or otherwise, is now in the hands of the free market. FT labelling initiatives may try to keep control of the movement, but in actual fact the battle has been long lost. They cleared the ground to benefit the major actors of agricultural value chains: they made the effort to sensitise consumers, to find 'champions' in many areas of the world where they instilled the values of the free market (quality, speed, efficiency, etc.) and *in fine* to prove that the 'sustainable' could be a profitable market. After unconsciously playing this watchdog role, the free market repaid itself by simply confiscating the benefits of the movement. It did so by taking over its champions and lifting the trade of 'ethical' products to unexpected heights. Within the coffee industry, for instance, Starbucks reported coffee purchases based on its own ethical standards of fair trading for an amount of £299 million in 2009, which represents seven times its own purchases of FT-certified coffee. So, Intensive Fair or Extensive Fair? *That is NOT the question.*

More broadly speaking, Fairtrade is not a sufficiently innovative and iconoclastic alternative. Its deference vis-à-vis the free market rationale is far too great to enable it to sustain the ambition of providing significant global change. Its approach runs counter to recent research according to which the countries that made it were those that dared to 'challenge' the free market by promoting exports which had previously seemed beyond their capacities as developing countries, and which they would never have been able to produce if they had complaisantly complied with the fallacious arguments of comparative advantage theory. The problem is therefore not whether Fair Trade is an idealistic project or a utopia. There is probably no harm in some measure of idealism or utopia when it is geared towards innovation and creativity. The problem lies with the outdated idealism which recommends the future strategy whereby developing countries continue to export, supposedly in their own interest, products that some of them have specialised in for centuries without gaining any positive and significant change in their living conditions. Recent history has shown that developing countries that managed to lift their economies largely focused on the export of manufactured products and on diversification.

For the sake of clarity, I shall point out that I do not advocate that LDCs turn away from agriculture. This would be of little consequence, as for some such countries, only a limited number of agricultural products account for export revenue. For countries in this situation, it is crucial in the first instance to facilitate market access and to (re)introduce income stabilisation mechanisms. Beyond this, enhancing agricultural productivity should generally be encouraged for a number of reasons. Through this approach, they would first and foremost ensure food sovereignty and security, especially in countries with dynamic demography.

This in turn can reduce the cost of food products for populations, alleviate the trade balance and facilitate a channelling of export revenue towards the import of basic intermediate goods. Refocusing agriculture around domestic concerns is, in my view, more profitablefor LDCs in the long term than an economic growth model based on agricultural exports.

In fact, in the framework of the discussions as part of the Doha round of multilateral negotiations, the Fairtrade experience described here could be considered as a very small-scale example of the possible distributive effects of liberalising agricultural product markets. Even though there may be positive gains for developing countries overall, these will probably only benefit a minority of them. For the vast majority of LDCs, import bills will undoubtedly increase. Hence the need to hold a consistent and transparent dialogue in order to address each other's specific needs.

This leads me to asking the following question: what should we do about Fairtrade? According to some authors, involving producers of the South further in decision-making instances would make the movement stronger. Others are rather in favour of making economic actors who join the movement more accountable. The most sceptical doubt the viability of the FT economic model, even while maintaining the illusion that it has a theoretical potential to offer. The movement would no doubt regain consistency and strengthen its local impact through a tighter bridging of Fairtrade and alternative Fair Trade as envisaged by the World Fair Trade Organization. At any rate, a critical redefinition of the guiding principles and the philosophy of the movement is needed. But whatever the nature or even the scope of such adjustments or reforms, one should not be under any illusions as to what the Fair Trade movement as a whole can achieve. The problems raised by globalisation today demand global and consistent solutions that take into account the diversity of contexts.

The Fair Trade movement took advantage of institutional and legal weaknesses, a testimony to the success of neoliberalism, to rise to the forefront. Today, its future is threatened by the same weaknesses that led to its birth. Therefore, the solution is not to grant FT labelling initiatives an international monopoly in terms of 'ethical' trade. On the contrary, it consists in making sure that the states regain the use of the regulatory powers they had delegated *nolens volens* to private initiatives. Indeed, the main and undeniable argument put forward by Fair Trade is that developing countries that export primary agricultural products should benefit from social safety mechanisms that would shield them from the tremors of the free market. Yet this need would no doubt better be taken into account if their governments had more room for manoeuvre from the political point of view.

In the case of the poorest countries, this political space tends to be increasingly reduced by 'governance'-related conditionality recommended by donors and embedded in multilateral and bilateral agreements discussed in various international fora. The challenge today is therefore to genuinely arrive at a new platform for global regulation that enables at once a strengthening and transcendence of some important initiatives – such as the Millennium Development Goals – which were suggested in order to better take into account the needs of the poorest countries.

In this book, the issues of international trade and of the injustices suffered by developing countries have been dealt with at length. However, this circumstantial position should in no way imply that the latter have no effort of their own to make. If only to fully benefit from the gains of economic openness, the poorest countries will have to consider the well-known *behind-the-border policies*, which consist in improving the quality of infrastructures, and rationalising administrative and customs procedures. This being said, the latter should not simply expect everything from international trade, although the latter could have a significant impact on their economies. Without a doubt, change must be driven from within the nation. In this increasingly complex world, the domestic fight for self-determination of the people and for better control of economic processes is, in my view, the cornerstone on which the poorest countries will have to build themselves up, as young nations aspiring to have their say in the global concert of nations.

Annexes

Table A1 Productivity statistics according to development level

	GDP per capita (current 2008 $)	GDP per capita, PPP* (constant 2005 $)	Agricultural value added per worker (constant 2000 $)
Low-income countries	490	1,114	285
Lower middle income	2,220	4,427	609
Upper middle income	8,389	13,052	3,681

Note: PPP = * Purchasing Power Parity.

Source: Development Indicators of the World Bank (2010a).

Table A2 Transfair USA's revenue compared to additional FT income transferred from USA (in thousand $)

	Licence fees	Total revenue	Total additional FT income from USA	FT premium	Receipts transferred*
2001	307	686	5,679	344	5,335
2002	474	1,114	8,121	518	7,603
2003	933	1,665	15,919	1,017	14,902
2004	1,895	2,748	26,624	2,061	24,563
2005	2,932	4,209	14,818	2,858	11,960
2006	4,521	5,570	17,770	4,037	13,733
2007	4,961	7,665	19,870	6,091	13,779
2008	5,757	9,270	34,671	10,811	23,860
2009	6,881	10,008	48,209	13,778	34,431

Note: * Additional income created by the positive differential between FT prices and market prices.

Source: Transfair USA (2009) and annual reports 2007–9.

Table A3 Transfair USA's revenue compared to additional FT income transferred from USA (in %)

	Licence fees/Receipts transferred*	Total income/Receipts transferred*
2001	5.8	12.9
2002	6.2	14.7
2003	6.3	11.2
2004	7.7	11.2
2005	24.5	35.2
2006	32.9	40.6
2007	36.0	55.6
2008	24.1	38.9
2009	20.0	29.1
Average 2001–9	19.0	28.6

Note: * Additional income created by the positive differential between FT prices and market prices.

Source: Table A2.

Table A4   International merchandise trade – structure by region in 2008 (in %)

	Food products	Agricultural raw materials	Ores, metals and precious stones	Fuels	Manufactured products	Total
Exports						
Africa	6.4	1.8	11.2	62.8	17.7	100
Latin America						
and Caribbean	17.8	2.0	12.7	23.4	42.8	100
Asia	4.2	1.0	3.9	19.4	69.2	100
Oceania	27.3	8.4	40.7	2.4	20.9	100
Imports						
Africa	13.8	1.5	3.9	14.1	64.2	100
Latin America						
and Caribbean	8.1	1.2	2.9	14.7	72.3	100
Asia	5.5	1.9	9.3	18.5	62.9	100
Oceania	19.1	0.7	0.9	21.8	55.1	100

Source: UNCTAD (2010b: Table 2.2, 84–107). Totals do not add to 100 due to numerous statistical sources used by UNCTAD.

Notes

Chapter 1

1. These are Brazil and Mexico for Latin America. For Asia, we have China, Taiwan, Hong Kong, the Republic of Korea, India, Malaysia, the Philippines, Singapore, Thailand and Turkey.
2. On this literature, see the pioneering work of Gereffi and Korzeniewicz (1994), as well as Kaplinski (2000), Humphrey and Memedovic (2006) and the FAO (2007).
3. The WTO distinguishes between export subsidies and other forms of domestic support to agriculture. It classifies the latter into several categories, according to whether or not they generate distortions in trade, and possibly according to the nature of such distortions. It seems that WTO rules are more indulgent towards domestic support measures other than export subsidies. In developed countries, the trend would seem to be the substitution of the latter by the former (Stiglitz and Charlton, 2005: 123–4).
4. According to the United Nations (2010: 66), net disbursements for official development assistance reached $119.6 billion in 2009.

Chapter 2

1. Available at: http://www.fairtrade-advocacy.org
2. Stabex is the acronym for the 'Export Revenue Stabilisation System'. Sysmin is the acronym for 'System for Minerals'. These two export revenue stabilisation mechanisms were enshrined in the Lomé Convention, a set of cooperation agreements between the European Union and ACP (Africa, the Caribbean and the Pacific) countries during the period 1975–2000. In 2000, the Cotonou Agreement replaced the Lomé Convention.
3. On this point, some authors criticise FLO for being at once judge and prosecutor. Jacquiau (2006), for instance, questions the independence of FLO-cert.
4. 'Shopping Choices can make a positive difference to farmers and workers in developing countries: Global Poll', article published on 11 October 2011 at: http://www.globescan.com
5. 'Fairtrade is the most widely recognized label globally', article published on 11 October 2011 on www.fairtrade.net
6. 'Ethical labels add millions to cost of food', article published in the *Daily Telegraph*, 11 October 2010.
7. 'Ethical label proliferation and competition cause concern', article published on 3 December 2010 at: http://www.foodnavigator.com/Financial-Industry/Ethical-label-proliferation-and-competition-cause-concern
8. Faced with this laissez-faire attitude, it is not surprising to notice some innovative initiatives such as 'halal cosmetics'.

Chapter 3

1. Drescher (1992), for instance, provides an excellent discussion on this point.

2. Drawing probably from the notion of 'carbon footprint', an American sustainable development organisation recently introduced a 'slavery footprint'. This indicator shows for instance how many 'men, women and children have to work' in order for consumers of the North to easily access common consumption goods such as denim trousers, MP3 players, etc. For further details, see: http://slaveryfootprint.org

3. Schumpeter (2006 [1954]: 179–80) wrote:

> But no matter what he actually learned or failed to learn from predecessors, the fact is that the *Wealth of Nations* does not contain a single *analytic* idea, principle, or method that was entirely new in 1776 [...].
> And it was Adam Smith's good fortune that he was thoroughly in sympathy with the humors of his time. He advocated the things that were in the offing, and he made his analysis serve them. Needless to insist on what this meant both for performance and success: where would the *Wealth of Nations* be without free trade and laissez-faire? Also, the 'unfeeling' or 'slothful' landlords who reap where they have not sown, the employers whose every meeting issues in conspiracy, the merchants who enjoy themselves and let their clerks and accountants do the work, and the poor laborers who support the rest of society in luxury – these are all important parts of the show. It has been held that A. Smith, far ahead of his time, braved unpopularity by giving expression to his social sympathies. This is not so. His sincerity I do not for a moment call into question. But those views were not unpopular. They were in fashion. A judiciously diluted Rousseauism is also evident in the equalitarian tendency of his economic sociology. (original italics)

4. See the debates between Alastair Smith (2008, 2009) and the Fairtrade Foundation on the one hand, and the neoliberal criticism of Fair Trade on the other (Brink, 2003; Griffith, 2009; Henderson, 2008; Haight and Henderson, 2010; Weber, 2007). Also see the bibliography in Mohan (2010) as well as Miller (2010) and Raynolds et al. (2007). Among writings by FT protagonists, we can mention Lamb (2009) and Bowes (2011), who, in addition to their advocacy, tell the story of Fair Trade and its historical precedents as a solidarity approach.

5. 'Un café plus cher, mais pas nécessairement plus équitable' [More expensive, but not necessarily fairer coffee], published on 25 September 2010. See : http://www.cyberpresse.ca/la-tribune/opinions

6. 'Le parlement européen appelle la commission européenne à encourager le commerce équitable dans les marchés publics' [The European Parliament asks the European Commission to Encourage Fair Trade in Public Procurement], published on 20 May 2010: http://www.oxfammagasinsdumonde.be/2010/05/le-parlement-europeen-appelle-la-commission-europeenne-a-encourager-le-commerce-equitable-dans-les-marches-publics/

7. See European Fair Trade Association, 'Case Study: Douwe Egberts vs. the Province of Groningen', http://www.fairprocurement.info/en/casestudies (accessed January 2013).

8. 'Douwe Egberts Coffee Is "Wrong" Fair Trade', published on 19 March 2010 at: http://www.dutchnews.nl

9. This comment is valid in the case of Fair Trade protagonists as well. For instance, an introduction to a book written by the former CEO of Max Havelaar France ends as follows: 'So let us not hold back! Let us buy Fair!' See Doussin (2009: 121).

10. *Economist* debates: 'Fair Trade: Statements', 7 May 2007, on the website of *The Economist* magazine. www.economist.com

11. The debate on the 'origins' of capitalism is highly controversial in Marxist literature. See on this issue Fine and Saad-Filho (2010), especially Chapter 6 and quoted references.

12. 'Walmart China Closes Chongqing Stores Amidst Pork Mislabeling Scandal', published on 10 October 2011 at: www.huffingtonpost.com

13. Organisations specialised in ethical labelling generally do not say a word about the fiscal practices of their clients. Many multinationals that claim to work for a 'fairer' world do not pay taxes either in producing countries or in consumer countries. Through tax havens, they are able to minimise their tax bill. For example, these practices are observed for the three largest companies that account for more than two-thirds of the global banana market: Dole, Chiquita and Fresh Del Monte. An investigation by *The Guardian* has shown that these three companies:

> had combined global sales of over $50bn (£24bn) in the last five years, and made $1.4bn of profits. They paid just $200m (or 14.3% of profits) in taxes between them in that period. In some years the banana companies have paid an effective tax rate as low as 8%, yet the standard rate of corporation tax in the US where they have their headquarters and file their accounts is 35%. (Griffiths and Lawrence, 2007)

14. Source: Sofres poll – 'Les Français et le Crommerce équitable (The French and Fair Trade) – conducted on 15 and 16 September 2010. National sample of 1,000 people representative of the whole population aged 18 and over (www.tns-sofres.com; accessed on October 2010).

Chapter 4

1. Dani Rodrik (2006) presents similar arguments in the case of China.

2. To paraphrase Keynes, who spoke of the 'euthanasia' of the 'rentier'.

3. The documentary entitled *Black Gold* shows that Ethiopian coffee producers prayed to God at one time so He would give them good prices, not knowing that this God was in the stock markets in London and New York, probably busy speculating. This is a good illustration of the commodity fetishism described by Marx.

4. For example, the UCIRI (the Spanish acronym for Unión de Comunidades Indígenas de la Región del Istmo – Union of Indigenous Communities of the Isthmus Region), Fair Trade 'champion' and *success story*, signed a ten-year contract with the Carrefour chain of supermarkets in 2002. This contract involves the payment of decent prices and compliance with specific requirements of Fair Trade. But it excludes independent certification by FLO-cert. In other words, the products of this Mexican cooperative are not sold under the Fairtrade label. The two co-founders of Fairtrade actually state:

> Ideally, Max Havelaar would want all Fair Trade products to bear its label: a fully understandable position from the point of view of Max Havelaar, its interest and the recognition of its work. But decisions must take into account the interests of coffee producers. From our point of view, a long-term relationship between Carrefour and Mexican cooperatives represents significant progress [...] In our opinion, it would be timely that, in light of current initiatives, those

who act in favour of Fair Trade take note of this development and adapt their policies to this reality. (Roozen and van der Hoff, 2002: 148)

5.   Today, I am concerned about the future of this trade, as multinationals attempt to create confusion by offering 'ethical' labels, products that are supposedly the result of durable or sustainable agriculture, or what not. But we have to understand that what multinationals label as 'sustainable' is in fact neither that for producers, nor for the land. (van der Hoff, 2005: 13)

6.   The methodology for the calculation of the minimum price and the cost of sustainable production is described in detail in FLO (2010a). This document will be used as a reference for the discussion that follows.

7.   'To estimate total labor costs for family labor and temporary hired labor the total number of mandays needed is multiplied by the local wage rate' (FLO, 2010a: 8). It should be pointed out that the document provides no specific information on child labour (should it be taken into account? If so, how should it be assessed? If not, why not?), while this phenomenon is often important in specific contexts where households are very poor. In principle, the 'sustainable cost' of the prohibition of child labour must be relatively high (the cost of replacing child labourers and of sending them to school).

8.   The FT minimum price was deflated on the basis of the consumer price index of the United States. The author justifies this choice by arguing that coffee prices are expressed in US dollars (Bacon, 2010). According to Jaffee (2009), inflation in coffee-producing countries was higher than that measured on the basis of the consumer price index of the United States.

9.   Otherwise, this approach would be illegal. Competition legislation in force in the United States and the European Union prohibits actors, such as labelling initiative organisations, from being involved in the price-setting mechanisms between importers and distribution networks (Mohan, 2010: 54).

10. In a summary document on impact evaluation studies produced by Max Havelaar France, the following is written on coffee: 'This chart helps to illustrate one of the mechanisms of LFT (Labelled Fair Trade), which guarantees a steady minimum price at times when prices are low, while the price is in line with international coffee prices when these are high. The price effect corresponds to the price differential and contributes to stabilising the income of producers' (Laroche and Guittard, 2009: 6).

11. It should also be pointed out that these charts fail to present the evolution of FT price in real terms. In most cases, this would likely present a completely different picture.

12. From a concrete point of view, FT household income is generally calculated by aggregating all sources: transfers, income from FT products, other agricultural income, non-agricultural income, etc. In principle, only the income mobilised as part of the FT production should be included in the comparison, unless it has had a demonstrable influence on other sources of income.

13. The following assumptions can be made: (1) producer organisations have limited access to land; (2) non-FT producers can sell their whole production at the market price, but do not have access to the FT market; (3) the share of unsold FT production on the FT market is sold at the market price; (4) the average cost of production for non-FT producers (Cm) is below the average cost of sustainable production (Cf), which in turn is inferior or equal to the FT price: $Cm < Cf \leq Pf$; (5) the conventional market price (> 0) can reach extreme values: it can be lower than the average production cost for non-FT producers; it can be higher than the

FT price; it can also lie anywhere between Cm and Pf. Let us point out that this discussion does not cover the issue of the relative quality of FT products. On this point, see for instance de Janvry et al. (2012).

14. If we take Mf as the FT unit margin (by definition ≥ 0) and Mm as the unit margin on the conventional market (which can take extreme values), we can identify four possibilities: (1) Mf > 0 and Mm > 0, (2) Mf = 0, (3) Mf > 0 and Mm = 0, (4) Mf > 0 and Mm < 0.

15. The phrase 'all things being equal' is justified, as the context must be taken into account. A high price is in principle a good thing for exporting producers. But it can also have a destabilising effect on local economies. For instance, when there is sustained foreign demand for specific products, local prices can increase as a result of the upsurge in international prices. To take the example of quinoa in Bolivia, an example not directly linked to Fair Trade, it would seem that the rise of its international price led to greater difficulty of access for populations who depended on this product for their subsistence. As a result, the spectre of malnutrition is looming close for the latter. See the *New York Times* article of 19 March 2011: 'Quinoa's Global Success Creates Quandary at Home', http://www.nytimes.com

16. We should point out that, since October 2011, FT producers hold 50 per cent of voting rights at the General Assembly of FT system actors. In the past, labelling initiatives had more weight than producers. See 'Producer Ownership of Fairtrade Moves to New Level', published on 14 October 2011: http://www.fairtrade.net

17. 'Flambée des cours des matières premières: le commerce équitable apporte-t-il des solutions?' [Soaring Raw Material Prices: Does Fair Trade Provide a Solution?], published on 10 March 2011: http://www.novethic.fr

18. See for instance the article in *La Tribune* of 8 July 2011: 'Alter Éco lance le Commerce équitable de proximité' [Alter Éco Launches Community Fair Trade]: http://www.latribune.fr

19. See for example 'Le Commerce équitable s'invite au G20' [Fair Trade Invites Itself to the G20], published on 5 May 2011: http://www.developpementdurable.com; also see the article published in *Le Monde* of 16 May 2011, by Jean-Pierre Doussin and Christophe Roturier, 'Messieurs du G20, pourquoi ne pas s'inspirer de l'exemple du Commerce équitable?' [Gentlemen of G20, Why Not Seek Inspiration in the Fair Trade Model?]: http://www.lemonde.fr

20. In descending order, these are: Colombia, Peru, Mexico, India, South Africa and Kenya. In 2011, this configuration remained unchanged. If we add Brazil, these countries contained 438 producer organisations out of a total of 1,030, or 42 per cent of the total (Transfair, 2011).

21. Specific monographs escape this criticism. Let us mention, for example, Jaffee (2007) and Fridell (2007) as far as FT coffee is concerned; Frundt (2009) for FT bananas; Lyon and Moberg (2010) list ethnographic studies on several products and countries.

22. The summary presented in Chapter 1 discusses the impact of Fair Trade on the environment and gender relations, and its externalities at the regional level. But its arguments are rather speculative, given the empirical focus of most studies in the book (production, income and consumption being the main themes discussed).

23. A recent impact study published by Max Havelaar France displays signs of the same bias. The three products focused on are coffee, bananas and cocoa. Organisations selected are all from four Latin American countries. They were chosen on the basis of two criteria: they had been involved in the FT system for

more than five years and had achieved a 'significant' level of sales for three years. This latter criterion invalidates in our mind the assumption that this study is representative of the situation of FT producers. See the summary compiled by Laroche and Guittard (2009).

24. Language can also be a non-trivial barrier in relations between producers and labelling organisations.

25. Jean-Pierre Doussin (2009: 107), the former Max Havelaar France chair, wrote:

> In the FLO/Max Havelaar system, the choice is clear: the organisations entering into the Fairtrade value chains should have the potential to become really autonomous, as the goal of FairTrade is to contribute to providing them with capability. This implies that two important elements are in place: actual internal dynamics and external support.

26. In Chapter 2 (Peru), the organisation of FT producers is part of a community of farmers that has existed since 1820, which includes 6,000 members and which is the *de jure* owner of community land. It is situated in an area where the state had started to promote the export of bananas since 1999. This translated into the granting of credit to purchase seeds and equipment for the packaging of products. In Chapter 4 (Costa Rica), the FT producer organisation selected was created in 1980. It has worked with a multinational for over 15 years (1980–95) on the basis of contractual terms including a price that covers production costs and the payment of wages to members of the producer cooperative. In Chapter 6 (Ghana), the FT group selected is a Ghanaian-Dutch joint venture created in 1988. In Chapter 7 (Ecuador), the FT group selected is the main Agrofair supplier as far as bananas is concerned. Their relation started in 1998.

27. For instance, in Chapter 5 of Ruben (2009), the two authors show that in the period 2004–7, a third of the FT premium was used to cover the FT certification renewal. The remainder, which was meant to be used for technological investments and technical support, was lower than the annual wage of a local agronomist.

28. As explained by a producer interviewed by Jaffee (2009: 214): 'The costs of production are going up, but the Fair Trade price has remained the same for ten years. Ten years ago, a mozo cost 20 pesos per day, but now they charge 50 pesos. Fair Trade really isn't fair anymore.'

29. Jaffee (2009) raises the possibility that this may result from under-reporting on the part of some households.

Chapter 5

1. Let us simply recall the conclusion that FT products generate more net gains for producers when these are also certified organic.

2. Articles published in newspapers such as the *Times* and the *Financial Times* backed this point of view. See Mohan (2010: 52–4).

3. By giving an average value to missing data, we come up with a total amount of €484 million. This does not in any way change the nature of the results presented below.

4. In an FLO evaluation report (2010c: 47–8, Table 12A), it is indicated that FT sales represented on average 61.7 and 30.7 per cent respectively of the total of sales by producer organisations and hired labour organisations. In the case of producer organisations, the rate of sale seems rather high given that normally found in various studies (see for example Mohan, 2010: 38–9). Besides, as these

are averages, we need to point out that they do not shed light on inequalities in terms of access to FT markets.

5. In the case of hired labour organisations, the destination of these earnings is *a priori* not straightforward since prices are negotiated by their employers who, in turn, are required to guarantee decent working conditions and wages to their employees.

6. See the FLO website and the 'Facts and figures' section especially. The Max Havelaar France 2009–10 annual report (Max Havelaar France, 2010: 14) places this figure at 8 million.

7. According to the World Bank development indicators (World Bank, 2010a), the average GDP per capita for LDCs was $692 in 2008, or €471 if we convert it at the average exchange rate between these two currencies in the year 2008. See the European Central Bank website: http://www.ecb.int/stats/exchange

8. In order to determine the net revenue from the FT production share sold at FT trading conditions, we could have used a 15 per cent margin rate assumption. But we decided not to present results which, though plausible, might represent a weakness that can easily be exploited. As we have seen in the previous chapter, this rate is provided as an example in the methodological document on the calculation of the FT minimum price, which is applied to the cost of sustainable production (FLO, 2010a). This is also the rate chosen by FLO in the framework of the *easy entry procedure* (FLO, 2010b).

9. Transfair USA (2009: 2–3) estimated the FT premium at $10.8 million in 2008. Let us point out that Transfair USA recently changed its trade name to Fair Trade USA.

10. According to the Transfair USA 2008 Annual Report (Transfair, 2008: 30), FT sales reached $1.25 billion in 2008. An article published on 14 October 2009 updates this amount at $1.1 billion. It is entitled 'How Deep Is Consumer Demand for Fairtrade?' (see: http://www.fairtraderesource.org/2009/10/14/how-deep-is-consumer-demand-for-fair-trade); this information is consistent with FLO data (FLO, 2009b: 23), which estimated FT sales on the American market at €758 million in 2008.

11. Additional income received by coffee producers is estimated at $32.6 million in 2008. See Transfair USA (2009: 2–3).

12. We were unable to provide a budget estimate for all labelling initiatives, as annual reports were only occasionally accessible online, not to mention the language barrier (reports are seldom translated into several languages).

13. Let us point out that Transfair USA, now Fair Trade USA, stopped being a member of FLO at the end of December 2011. See 'Joint Announcement from Fairtrade International and Fair Trade USA', published on 15 September 2011 at: http://www.fairtrade.net

14. 'Upper middle-income countries' (a category that mainly includes Latin American countries) have a level of agricultural productivity that is 6 to 13 times higher than that of lower middle-income countries and low-income countries. See Box 1.1 on developing countries for a description of this typology. Data on agricultural productivity is from World Bank (2010a). See Table A1 in the Annexes.

15. All the statistics pertaining to FT certification are derived from FLO (2010e).

16. These figures are based on FLO (2010c: 51–2).

17. In 2008, the GDP per capita of France was 4.4 times higher than that of Mexico. The GDP per capita of Mexico on the other hand was 14 times higher than the average GDP per capita of LDCs (World Bank, 2010a; GDP per capita in current $).

18. For coffee, the bias in the certification offer has not changed. See Transfair USA (2011: 18).

19. As far as LDCs are concerned, UNCTAD (2010a) notes that in this booming period, the value of food product imports rose from $7.6 billion in 2000 to $24.8 billion in 2008.

20. For a review of this voluminous literature on models of gravity, see Fratianni (2009). For a more theoretical approach, see Anderson (2011).

21. According to the 2009 UNCTAD Handbook of Statistics (UNCTAD, 2010b: ch. 3.2.D, 163–80), the tenth most exported product would account for 2 per cent of export revenue in the case of South Africa, against 1.6 per cent in the case of India.

22. According to ILO, the share of labour employed in agriculture in 2008 was estimated at 61 per cent in sub-Saharan Africa against 17.4 per cent in Latin America and the Caribbean. For Asia, the corresponding figure is comprised between a minimum of 40.6 per cent for East Asia and a maximum of 47.7 per cent for South Asia. With regards to the proportion of wage workers, they are respectively 24.7 per cent for sub-Saharan Africa and 63.5 per cent for Latin America and the Caribbean. For Asia, the minimum is recorded in South Asia with 21.5 per cent against a maximum of 45.1 per cent for East Asia. See the documents attached to the Key Indicators of the Labour Market 3 and 4 in ILO (2010).

23. In a Canadian documentary on water privatisation in developing countries – The Water Hold-Up, directed in 2006 by Neil Doherty – the economist Jeffrey Sachs was interviewed to comment on human tragedies caused by this policy. In essence, he said something like this : 'Even those with the best of intentions recognise that the market has failed because the poor are dying and that no one takes their needs into account.' After saying this, he makes an important clarification. According to him, the case of water privatisation is not an example of 'market failures' as this expression is usually understood by economists. He argues that the market 'has done its job very well', namely looking after people with an income and looking after their needs.

24. This is inspired by Milanovic (2006).

25. Not to mention, also, that producers in the South must pay an annual certification fee in order to receive help.

26. For Frans van der Hoff (2005: 136), one of the structural characteristics of neoliberalism is that 'it takes away money from the poorer social classes to give it to the wealthier social classes'.

27. The economist and historian Jeffrey Williamson, as well as many of his colleagues, distinguish a first 'wave' of globalisation, which they place between 1870 and 1913 and refer to as the 'age of mass migration'. In contrast, the second 'wave' of globalisation would have started in the 1950s and continues to the present. From their point of view, the intervening period (1913–45) would be one of de-globalisation. See for example Williamson (1996).

28. According to Rodrik (2007b: 8), with a 3 per cent increase in their share of the labour force of rich countries, immigrants from the South would enjoy net gains of $265 billion per year. This is considerably higher than gain estimates as part of the Doha round of negotiations ($30 billion according to Rodrik).

29. Denmark, Luxembourg, the Netherlands, Norway and Sweden are the five countries that reached this target of 0.7 per cent of their Gross National Income in 2009 (United Nations, 2010).

Conclusion

1. Here are two quotes to illustrate this statement further. First: 'We are as opposed to state intervention as we are to neoliberal economy and we offer, instead, a sustainable social economy' (van der Hoff, 2005: 140–1). Then: 'We can learn from the past. State intervention in the production sector leads to waste, corruption and inefficiency. This is why a modern government should encourage the private sector' (Roozen and van der Hoff, 2002: 252).
2. In 2008, commodity exports from developing countries were structured as follows: 48.8 per cent for South–South trade against 46.7 per cent for North–South trade. For imports, these amounted to 55.5 per cent for South–South trade against 40.8 per cent for North–South trade. See the *UNCTAD Handbook of Statistics, 2009* (2010b: 80–3). It is to be pointed out that Asia is at once the largest exporter and the largest importer of South–South trade. This explains the widespread use of the phrase '*hub and spoke* network' to describe the nature of these trade flows.

Bibliography

Actionaid (2007) 'Who Pays? How British Supermarkets Are Keeping Women and Workers in Poverty', April (www.actionaid.org/uk, accessed August 2013).

Alexander, Jeffrey C. (1987) *Twenty Lectures: Sociological Theory since World War 2* (New York: Columbia University Press).

Anderson, James E. (2011) 'The Gravity Model', *Annual Review of Economics*, 3(1): 133–60.

Bacon, Christopher M. (2010) 'Who Decides What Is Fair in Fair Trade? The Agri-Environmental Governance of Standards, Access, and Price', *Journal of Peasant Studies*, 37(1): 111–47.

Bairoch, Paul (1995 [1993]) *Economics and World History: Myths and Paradoxes* (Chicago: University of Chicago Press).

Ballet, Jêrome and Carimentrand, Aurélie (2007) *Le Commerce équitable* [*Fair Trade*] (Paris: Ellipses).

Bardhan, Kalpana (1977) 'Rural Employment and Wages with Agricultural Growth in India: Intertemporal and Cross-sectional Study', Berkeley, Department of Economics, University of California.

Bateman, Milford (2010) *Why Doesn't Microfinance Work? The Destructive Rise of Local Neoliberalism* (London: Zed Books).

Berndt, Colleen E.H. (2007) 'Does Fair Trade Coffee Help the Poor? Evidence from Costa Rica and Guatemala', *Policy Comment no. 1*, Mercatus Center, George Mason University.

Bhagwati, Jagdish (2008) *Termites in the Trading System: How Preferential Agreements Undermine Free Trade* (New York: Oxford University Press).

Booth, Philip (2008) 'The Economics of Fair Trade: A Christian Perspective', Institute of Economic Affairs (www.iea.org.uk, accessed August 2013).

Boris, Jean-Pierre (2005) *Commerce inéquitable: le roman noir des matières premières* [*Unfair Trade: The Dark Story of Raw Materials*] (Paris: Hachette littératures).

Bouët, Antoine (2008) 'The Expected Benefits of Trade Liberalization for World Income and Development. Opening the "Black Box" of Global Trade Modelling', *Food Policy Review* 8 (Washington, DC: International Food Policy Research Institute).

Bowes, John (2011) *The Fair Trade Revolution* (London: Pluto Press).

Brenner, Robert (1977) 'The Origins of Capitalist Development: a Critique of Neo-Smithian Marxism', *New Left Review* 104: 25–92.

Brink, Lindsey (2003) 'Grounds for Complaint? Understanding the "Coffee Crisis"', Center for Trade Policy Studies, *Trade Briefing Paper* no. 16, May, Washington, DC: Cato Institute.

Brown, Michael B. (1993) *Fair Trade: Reform and Realities in the International Trading System* (London: Zed Books).

Bureau, Jean-Christophe, Jean, Sebastian and Matthews, Alan (2006) 'The Consequences of Agricultural Trade Liberalization for Developing Countries: Distinguishing Between Genuine Benefits and False Hopes', *World Trade Review* 5(2): 225–49.

Chang, Ha-Joon (2002) *Kicking Away the Ladder: Development Strategy in Historical Perspective* (London: Anthem Press).

Chang, Ha-Joon (2008) *Bad Samaritans: The Myth of Free Trade and the Secret History of Capitalism* (New York: Bloomsbury Press).

Daviron, Benoit and Ponte, Stefano (2005) *The Coffee Paradox: Global Markets, Commodity Trade and the Elusive Promise of Development* (London: Zed Books).

De Janvry, Alain, Mcintosh, Craig and Sadoulet, Elisabeth (2012) 'Fair Trade and Free Entry: Can a Disequilibrium Market Serve a Development Tool?', September, (http://irps.ucsd.edu/assets/001/503924.pdf, accessed December 2012).

Demaze, Moïse T. (2008) 'Quand le développement prime sur l'environnement: la déforestation en Amazonie brésilienne' [When Development Prevails over the Environment: The Case of Deforestation in the Amazonian Rainforest of Brazil], *Mondes en Développement*, 143: 1–22.

Diao, Xinshen, Díaz-Bonilla, Eugenio and Robinson, Sherman (2003) *How Much Does It Hurt? The Impact of Agricultural Trade Policies on Developing Countries* (Washington, DC: International Food Policy Research Institute).

Doussin, Jean-Pierre (2009) *Le Commerce équitable* [Fair Trade] (Paris: PUF, Que sais-je ?).

Drescher, Seymour (1992) 'The Ending of Slave Trade and the Evolution of European Scientific Racism', in Inikori, Joseph E. and Engerman, Stanley L. (eds) *The Atlantic Slave Trade: Effects on Economies, Societies and Peoples in Africa, the Americas and Europe* (Durham, NC: Duke University Press, 361–96).

Duménil, Gérard and Lévy, Dominique (2011) *The Crisis of Neoliberalism* (Cambridge, MA: Harvard University Press).

Elliott, Kimberly A. (2010) *Open Markets for the Poorest Countries: Trade Preferences that Work*. Report of the Center for Global Development Working Group on Global Trade Preference Reform. Final Report, April (www.cgdev.org, accessed August 2010).

Ellis, Karen and Keane, Jodie (2008) 'A Review of Ethical Standards and Labels: Is There a Gap in the Market for a New "Good for Development" Label?' *Working Paper 297* (London: Overseas Development Institute).

Emmanuel, Arghiri (1972 [1969]) *Unequal Exchange: A Study of the Imperialism of Trade* (translated from French. New York: Monthly Review Press).

Esping-Andersen, Gøsta (1990) *The Three Worlds of Welfare Capitalism* (Princeton, NJ: Princeton University Press).

European Commission (1997) 'Attitudes of EU Consumers to Fair Trade Bananas', *Eurobarometer Survey* no. 47 (http://ec.europa.eu/public_opinion/archives/eb_special_120_100_en.htm, accessed August 2010).

FAO (Food and Agriculture Organization) (2004) *The State of Agricultural Commodity Markets 2004* (Rome: FAO).

FAO (Food and Agriculture Organization) (2006) *The State of Agricultural Commodity Markets 2006* (Rome: FAO).

FAO (Food and Agriculture Organization) (2007) *Governance, Coordination and Distribution along Commodity Value Chains*. FAO Commodities and Trade Proceedings 2, 4–5 April 2006 (Rome, FAO).

FAO (Food and Agriculture Organization) (2009) *The State of Agricultural Commodity Markets 2009: High food Prices and the Food Crises – Experience and Lessons Learned* (Rome: FAO).

FAO (Food and Agriculture Organization) (2010) 'List and Definition of Low-Income Food Deficit Countries' (http://www.fao.org/countryprofiles/lifdc/en; accessed on December 2010).

Feenstra, Robert (1998) 'Integration of Trade and Disintegration of Production in the Global Economy', *Journal of Economic Perspectives*, 12(4): 31–50.

Fine, Ben and Leopold, Ellen (2002) *The World of Consumption: The Material and Cultural Revisited*, 2nd edn (London: Routledge).

Fine, Ben and Saad-Filho, Alfredo (2010) *Marx's Capital*, 5th edn (London: Pluto Press).

FLO (Fairtrade Labelling Organizations International) (2009) *Annual Report 2008/2009: Fairtrade Leading the Way* (Bonn: FLO).

FLO (Fairtrade Labelling Organizations International) (2010a) 'Guideline for Estimating Costs of Sustainable Production, Pricing Subunit', 26 March (Bonn: FLO).

FLO (Fairtrade Labelling Organizations International) (2010b) 'Standard Operating Procedure Development of Fairtrade Minimum Prices and Premiums', 31 March (Bonn: FLO).

FLO (Fairtrade Labelling Organizations International) (2010c) *The Benefits of Fairtrade, second edition. A Monitoring and Evaluation Report of Fairtrade Certified Producers' Organizations for 2008*. August (Bonn: FLO).

FLO (Fairtrade Labelling Organizations International) (2010d) *Annual Report 2009–2010: Growing Stronger Together* (Bonn: FLO).

FLO (Fairtrade Labelling Organizations International) (2010e) 'Producer Evolution for Year 2009', version 01, March (Bonn: FLO).

FLO (Fairtrade Labelling Organizations International) (2011) *Monitoring the Scope and Benefits of Fairtrade*, 3rd edn (Bonn: FLO).

FLO (Fairtrade Labelling Organizations International) (2012) *Annual Report 2011–2012: For Producers, With Producers* (Bonn: FLO) (www.fairtrade.net, accessed April 2012).

Fratianni, Michèle (2009) 'The Gravity Equation in International Trade', in A. Rugman (eds) *The Oxford Handbook of International Business* (New York: Oxford University Press, 72–89).

Fridell, Gavin (2007) *Fair Trade Coffee: The Prospects and Pitfalls of Market-driven Social Justice* (Toronto: University of Toronto Press).

Frundt, Henry (2009) *Fair Bananas! Farmers, Workers and Consumers Strive to Change an Industry* (Tucson: University of Arizona Press).

Georgescu-Roegen, Nicholas (1995 [1979]) *La* Décroissance*: entropie–écologie–économie [Degrowth : Entropy–Ecology–Economy]* (Paris: Éditions Sang de la Terre).

Gereffi, Gary and Korzeniewicz, Miguel (eds) (1994) *Commodity Chains and Global Capitalism* (London: Praeger).

Gereffi, Gary, Humphrey, John and Sturgeon, Timothy (2005) 'The Governance of Global Value Chains', *Review of International Political Economy*, 12(1): 78–104.

Getz, Christy and Shreck, Aimee (2006) 'What Organic and Fair Trade Labels do Not Tell Us: Towards a Place-based Understanding of Certification', *International Journal of Consumer Studies*, 30(5): 490–501.

GFN (Global Footprint Network) (2010) *The Ecological Wealth of Nations* (www.footprintnetwork.org, accessed August 2013).

Griffith, Peter (2009) 'Lack of Rigour in Defending Fairtrade: A Reply to Alastair Smith', *Economic Affairs*, 30(2): 45–9.

Griffiths, Ian and Lawrence, Felicity (2007) 'Bananas to UK via the Channel Islands? It Pays for Tax Reasons', *The Guardian*, 6 November.

Guerrien, Bernard (1999) *La Théorie économique néoclassique, 1: Microéconomie [Neoclassical Economic Theory, 1: Microeconomics]* (Paris: La Découverte).

Guthman, Julie (2007) 'The Polanyian Way? Voluntary Food Labels as Neoliberal Governance', *Antipode*, 39(3): 456–78.

Haight, Colleen and Henderson, David R. (2010) 'Fair Trade is Counterproductive and Unfair: Rejoinder', *Institute of Economic Affairs*, 30(1): 88–91.

Harvey, David (2005) *A Brief History of Neoliberalism* (New York: Oxford University Press).

Henderson, David R. (2008) 'Fair Trade is Counterproductive and Unfair', *Economic Affairs*, 28(3): 62–4.

Hoekman, Bernard, Ng, Francis and Olarreaga, Marcelo (2004) 'Agricultural Tariffs or Subsidies: Which Are More Important for Developing Countries?', *World Bank Economic Review*, 18(2): 175–204.

Howell, George (2007) 'The North–Southern Environmental Crisis: An Unequal Ecological Exchange Analysis', *New School Economic Review*, 2(1): 77–99.

Hudson, Ian, Hudson, Mark and Fridell, Mara (2013) *Fair Trade, Sustainability and Social Change* (Houndmills: Palgrave Macmillan).

Hudson, Michael W. (2009) *Trade, Development and Foreign Debt*, new edition (New York: ISLET).

Humphrey, John and Memedovic, Olga (2006) 'Global Value Chains in the Agrifood Sector', Working Paper (Vienna: United Nations Industrial Development Organization).

ILO (International Labour Organization) (2010) 'Key Indicators of Labour Market' (www.ilo.kilm.org, accessed August 2010).

Jacquiau, Christian (2006) *Les Coulisses du commerce équitable: mensonges et vérités sur un petit business qui monte* [Behind the Scenes of Fair Trade: The Truths and the Lies Regarding a Small Business that Rises] (Paris: Mille et une Nuits).

Jaffee, Daniel (2007) *Brewing Justice: Fair Trade Coffee, Sustainability and Survival* (Berkeley: University of California Press).

Jaffee, Daniel (2009) '"Better, But Not Great": The Social and Environmental Benefits and Limitations of Fair Trade for Indigenous Coffee Producers in Oaxaca, Mexico', in R. Ruben (eds) *The Impact of Fair Trade* (The Netherlands: Wageningen Academic Publishers).

Jorgenson, Andrew K. and Rice, James (2005) 'Structural Dynamics of International Trade and Material Consumption: A Cross-national Study of Ecological Footprints of the Less-developed Countries', *Journal of World-Systems Research*, 11(1): 57–77.

Kaimowitz, David, Mertens, Benoit, Wunder, Sven and Pacheco, Pablo (2004) *Hamburger Connection Fuels Amazon Destruction: Cattle Ranching and Deforestation in Brazil's Amazon*, Technical Report (Indonesia: Center for International Forest Research, Bogor, http://www.cifor.cgiar.org, accessed August 2013).

Kaplinski, Raphael (2000) 'Globalization and Unequalization: What Can be Learned from Global Value Chain Analysis', *Journal of Development Studies*, 37(2): 117–46.

Karpyta, Frédéric (2009) *La Face cachée du Commerce équitable: comment le business fait main basse sur une idée généreuse* [The Hidden Face of Fair Trade: How the Business is Ripping Off a Generous Idea] (Paris: Bourin éditeur).

Keynes, John M. (1973 [1934]) 'Poverty in Plenty: Is the Economic System Self-adjusting?', in *The Collected Writings of John Maynard Keynes*, vol. 13 (London: Macmillan/St Martin's Press).

Klein, Naomi (2000) *No Logo: Taking Aim at the Brand Bullies* (London: Picador).

Krier, Jean-Marie (2008) *Fair Trade 2007: New Facts and Figures for an Ongoing Success Story. A Report on Fair Trade in 33 Consuming Countries.* Survey Prepared on Behalf of DAWS – Dutch Association of Worldshops, the Netherlands.

Lamb, Harriet (2009) *Fighting the Banana Wars and other Fair Trade Battles* (UK: Random House).

Laroche, Karine and Guittard, Barbara (2009) *L'Impact du Commerce équitable labellisé: bilan des premières études réalisées* [*The Impact of Labelled Fair Trade: An Assessment of Initial Studies*] (April, Max Havelaar France: www.maxhavelaarfrance.org, accessed August 2011).

Latouche, Serge (2004) *Survivre au développement: de la déconstruction de l'imaginaire économique à la construction d'une société alternative* [*Surviving Development: From Deconstructing the Economic Imaginary to Building an Alternative Society*] (Paris: Mille et une Nuits).

List, Friedrich (1885 [1841]) *National System of Political Economy* (translated from German by Sampson S. Lloyd. London: Longmans, Green, and Co.).

Lyon, Sarah and Moberg, Mark (eds) (2010) *Fair Trade and Social Justice: Global Ethnographies* (New York: New York University Press).

Magnusson, Lars (2004) *The Tradition of Free Trade* (London: Routledge, Taylor & Francis Group).

Marx, Karl (1887 [1867]) *Capital. A Critique of Political Economy. Book 1*, (http://www.marxists.org/archive/marx/works/1867-c1/, accessed January 2013).

Max Havelaar France (2010) *Rapport Annuel 2009–2010* [*Annual Report 2009–2010*] (www.maxhavelaarfrance.org, accessed September 2010).

Mayda, Anna Maria, O'Rourke, H. Kevin and Sinnott, Richard (2007) 'Risk, Government and Globalization: International Survey Evidence', *Working Paper 13037* (Cambridge, MA: National Bureau of Economic Research).

Michalet, Charles-Albert (2004) *Qu'est-ce que la mondialisation? Petit traité à l'usage de ceux et celles qui ne savent pas encore s'il faut être pour ou contre* [*What is Globalisation? A Short Treatise for Those Who Haven't Yet Made Up Their Minds*] (Paris: La Découverte).

Milanovic, Branko (2006) 'Global Income Inequality: What It Is and Why It Matters', *World Economics* 7(1): 131–57.

Milanovic, Branko (2010) *The Haves and the Have-Nots: A Brief and Idiosyncratic History of Global Inequality* (New York: Basic Books).

Miller, Debra A. (eds) (2010) *Fair Trade* (Current Controversies series; Farmington Hills, MI: Greenhaven Press).

Mirowski, Philip and Plehwe, Dieter (eds) (2009) *The Road from Mont Pelerin: The Making of the Neoliberal Thought Collective* (Cambridge, MA: Harvard University Press).

Mohan, Sushil (2010) *Fairtrade without the Froth: A Dispassionate Economic Analysis of 'Fair Trade'* (London: Institute of Economic Affairs).

Muradian, Roldan and Martinez-Alier, Joan (2001) 'Trade and the Environment: From a "Southern" Perspective', *Ecological Economics* 36: 281–97.

Myers, Gordon (2004) *Banana Wars. The Price of Free Trade* (London: Zed Books).

Myers, Norman (1981) 'The Hamburger Connection: How Central America's Forests Become North America's Hamburgers', *Ambio*, 10(1): 2–8.

Nadel, Henri (1994) *Marx et le Salariat* [*Marx and the Wage Employment Nexus*] (Paris: L'Harmattan).

Nelson, Valerie and Pound, Barry (2009) *The Last Ten Years: A Comprehensive Review of the Literature on the Impact of Fairtrade* (London: Natural Resource Institute, University of Greenwich: www.fairtrade.org/uk, accessed August 2010).

OECD (2008) 'Agricultural Support: How Is It Measured and What Does It Mean?' (Paris: OECD, http://www.oecd.org/tad/agriculturalpoliciesandsupport/44924550.pdf, accessed January 2013).

OECD (2010) *Agricultural Policies in OECD Countries: At a Glance* (Paris: OECD).

Oman, Charles P. and Wignaraja, Ganeshan (1991) *Postwar Evolution of Development Thinking* (Houndmills: Palgrave Macmillan).

Oxfam (2002) *Rigged Rules and Double Standards: Trade, Globalization and the Fight against Poverty* (Oxford: Oxfam International).

Oxfam (2004) '"White Gold" Turns to Dust: Which Way Forward for Cotton in West Africa?', Oxfam Briefing Paper 58 (Oxford: Oxfam International).

Pedregal, Virginie D. (2006) 'Le Développement du Commerce équitable: une menace pour l'environnement ?' [Is the Development of Fair Trade an Environmental Threat?], 2nd International Colloquium on Fair Trade and Sustainable Development, 19–21 June, Montréal, Quebec.

Pedregal, Virginie D. (2007) *Le Commerce équitable dans la France contemporaine: ideologies et pratiques* [*Fair Trade in Contemporary France: Ideology and Practice*] (Paris: L'Harmattan).

Penson, Jonathan (2007) 'Fairtrade or Fifty-Fifty: The Consequences of Shifts in African Perceptions of Fairtrade for Development Education Practitioners', *Policy & Practice: A Development Education Review*, 5: 20–30.

Philips, Jos (2009) 'Is There a Moral Case for Fair Trade Products? On the Moral Duty for Consumers to Buy and for Governments to Support Fair Trade Products', in R. Ruben (ed.) *The Impact of Fair Trade*, 2nd edn (The Netherlands: Wageningen Academic Publishers).

Polanyi, Karl (2001 [1944]) *The Great Transformation: The Political and Economic Origins of Our Time*, 2nd edn (Boston, MA: Beacon Press).

Popper, Karl (1970) 'Normal Science and its Dangers', in Lakatos, I. and Musgrave, A. (eds) *Criticism and the Growth of Knowledge* (Cambridge: Cambridge University Press).

Pritchett, Lant (2006) *Let Their People Come: Breaking the Gridlock on Global Labour Mobility* (Washington, DC: Center for Global Development).

Progressive Policy Institute (2002) 'America's Hidden Tax on the Poor: The Case for Reforming US Tariff Policy' (March, Washington, DC: Progressive Policy Institute).

Ratha, Dilip and Mohaptra, Sanket (2007) 'Increasing the Macroeconomic Impact of Remittances on Development, Development Prospect Groups' (Washington, DC: World Bank).

Raynolds, Laura T., Murray, Douglas and Wilkinson, John (2007) *Fair Trade: The Challenges of Transforming Globalization* (London: Routledge).

Renard, Marie-Christine (2003) 'Fair Trade: Quality, Market and Conventions', *Journal of Rural Studies* 19: 87–96.

Rist, Gilbert (2006 [1996]) *The History of Development: From Western Origins to Global Faith*, 2nd edn (London: Zed Books).

Rodriguez, Francisco and Rodrik, Dani (2000) 'Trade Policy and Economic Growth: A Skeptic's Guide to the Cross-national Evidence', *NBER Macroeconomics Annual 2000*, 15: 261–338.

Rodrik, Dani (1998) 'Why do More Open Economies Have Bigger Governments?', *Journal of Political Economy*, 106 (5): 997–1032.

Rodrik, Dani (2006) 'What's So Special about China's Exports?' China and World Economy, Institute of World Economics and Politics, *Chinese Academy of Social Sciences* 14(5): 1–19.

Rodrik, Dani (2007a) *One Economics, Many Recipes: Globalization, Institutions and Economic Growth* (Princeton, NJ: Princeton University Press).

Rodrik, Dani (2007b) 'How to Save Globalization from its Cheerleaders', *Journal of International Trade and Diplomacy*, 1(2): 1–33.

Roozen, Nico and van der Hoff, Frans (2002) *L'Aventure du Commerce équitable: une alternative à la mondialisation* [*The Fair Trade Journey: An Alternative to Globalization*] (Paris: Éditions Jean-Claude Lattès, for the French translation).

Ruben, Ruerd (ed.) (2009) *The Impact of Fair Trade*, 2nd edn (The Netherlands: Wageningen Academic Publishers).

Schumpeter, Joseph A. (2006 [1954]) *History of Economic Analysis*, revised edn, introduction by Mark Perlman (Oxford: Oxford University Press).

Schütz, Helmut, Moll, Stephan and Bringezu, Stefan (2004) 'Globalization and the Shifting Environmental Burden: Material Trade Flows of the European Union', *Wuppertal Papers* no.134e, July (Wuppertal: Wuppertal Institute for Climate, Environment, Energy).

Sharif, Mohammed (2000) 'Inverted "S" – The Complete Neoclassical Labour Supply Function', *International Labour Review*, 139(4): 409–35.

Sidwell, Marc (2008) 'Unfair Trade' (London: Adam Smith Institute, http://www.adamsmith.org /images/ pdf/unfair_trade.pdf, accessed August 2010).

Smith, Alastair M. (2008) 'A Response to the Adam Smith Report and a New Way to Think about Measuring the Content of the Fair Trade Cup' (Cardiff: Cardiff University: http://papers.ssrn.com/sol3/papers.cfm?abstract_id=1543903, accessed August 2013).

Smith, Alastair M. (2009) 'Evaluating the Criticisms of Fair Trade', *Economic Affairs* 29(4): 29–36.

Steger, Manfred B. and Roy, Ravi K. (2010) *Neoliberalism: A Very Short Introduction* (New York: Oxford University Press).

Stiglitz, Joseph E. and Charlton, Andrew (2005) *Fair Trade for All: How Trade Can Promote Development* (New York: Oxford University Press).

Transfair USA (2008) *Celebrating 10 Years: Transfair USA 2008 Annual Report* (Oakland, CA: Transfair USA).

Transfair USA (2009) *Almanac 2009* (Oakland, CA: Transfair USA).

Transfair USA (2011) *Almanac 2011* (Oakland, CA: Transfair USA) (http://www.fairtradeusa.org/resource-library/downloads, accessed April 2012).

UN Comtrade (2010) Online database: Country Profile 2009 (http://comtrade.un.org/pb/CountryPagesNew.aspx?y=2009, accessed December 2010).

UNCTAD (2008a) *Trade and Development Report: Commodity Prices, Capital Flows and the Financing of Investment* (New York: United Nations).

UNCTAD (2008b) *Cocoa: Industry Structures and Competition* (New York: United Nations).

UNCTAD (2009) *Trade and Development Report: Responding to the Global Crisis – Climate Change Mitigation and Development* (New York: United Nations).

UNCTAD (2010a) *The Least Developed Countries 2010: Towards a New International Development Architecture for LDCs* (New York: United Nations).

UNCTAD (2010b) *UNCTAD Handbook of Statistics 2009* (New York: United Nations) (see also the online database: http://stats.unctad.org /Handbook, accessed August 2010).

UNDP (UN Development Programme) (2009) *World Report on Human Development 2010. Overcoming barriers: Human Mobility and Development* (New York: UNDP).

United Nations (2006) *International Migration and Development*. Report of the Secretary General, May (New York: United Nations).

United Nations (2010) *Millennium Development Goals: 2010 Report* (New York, United Nations).

Van der Hoff, Frans (2005) *Nous ferons un monde équitable* [*We Will Create a Fair World*] (Paris: Flammarion).

Weber, Jeremy (2007) 'Fair Trade Coffee Enthusiasts Should Confront Reality', *Cato Journal* 27(1): 109–17.

Williams, Eric (1994 [1944]) *Capitalism and Slavery* (Chapel Hill, NC: University of North Carolina Press).

Williamson, Jeffrey G. (1996) 'Globalization, Convergence and History', *Journal of Economic History*, 56 (2): 277–306.

World Bank (2000) *Can Africa Claim the 21st Century?* (Washington, DC: World Bank).

World Bank (2002) *Global Economic Prospects and the Developing Countries* (Washington, DC: World Bank).

World Bank (2010a) 'World Development Indicators online database' (http://databank.worldbank.org, accessed August 2010).

World Bank (2010b) *Connecting to Compete. Trade Logistics in the Global Economy – The Logistics Performance Index and its Indicators* (Washington, DC: World Bank).

World Bank and International Monetary Fund (2008) *Global Monitoring Report 2008. MDGs and the Environment: Agenda for Inclusive and Sustainable Development* (Washington, DC: World Bank).

World Bank and International Monetary Fund (2009) *Global Monitoring Report 2009: A Development Emergency* (Washington, DC: World Bank).

WTO (World Trade Organization) (2003) *Annual Report 2003* (Geneva: WTO).

WTO (World Trade Organization) (2009) *International Trade Statistics* (Geneva: WTO).

WTO (World Trade Organization) (2010) 'Online Database: Times Series on International Trade' (http://stat.wto.org/, accessed December 2010).

Index